Erasmus and a Portrait of Thomas More

By Holbein

All is One

Introduction

There is a life size group portrait of Thomas More and his family, now owned by the National Trust which I think is probably the greatest artwork ever produced. Why would I suggest this?

The message written in the portrait represents peaceful nonviolent pacifism including human rights, particularly women's rights and a type of new learning called devotio-moderna all of which for the sixteenth century make it the greatest artwork ever produced. Think of all the human struggles that have taken place in the last five hundred years and here is a work of art screaming at the top of its voice stop gentlemen this is madness, put all of your guns down, take a good look at yourselves you are all mad led by the madder still.

Thomas More and his humanist friend Erasmus both avidly encouraged the study of philosophy. For these reasons we will be taking a closer look into the most notable philosophies of Aristotle and Plato including their influences over the Renaissance and Reformation periods.

To help us grasp the reasons why the Renaissance and subsequent Reformation transformed the Medieval age there can be no finer example in art than the More family portrait. The family have been carefully arranged and the scene is clearly staged to show they are absorbed with the new learning that removed us from those dark ages.

For this reason, I have chosen to use the book to serve a secondary purpose by way of an introduction to philosophy, which simply means *"the lover of wisdom"*. This secondary purpose naturally must identify what wisdom truly means otherwise we would be like the blind leading the blind.

But who was the artist? who commissioned the portrait? When was it done? The answer is there is no one who knows, it is a mystery and we are going to see if we can solve it.

I hope you will enjoy the book; I have tried to keep it simple, philosophical concepts can be difficult to grasp sometimes even demanding a great deal of mental effort and for this reason you may even consider I get too deep, but I can assure your patience will be rewarded. With my wisdom I will try to keep your interest attentive, adding a little humour here and there which will make it fun and easy. Socrates said learning should never be forced so if you are new to philosophy allow your mind time to relax and contemplate appreciating the ideas rather than rushing along you will surprise yourself. My tip is to relax and let the brain muscle work for you this is a different way of thinking than you will have come across before, but thankfully there is a growing interest in this right thinking, just enjoy.

By the way introductions can be so misleading, things are always better for knowing simply this is a book that challenges the wrong kind of thinking which we all have from time to time.

Come along with me and see if we can discover the true sources of all the misguided conflicts.

With the very best of wishes

To the illustrious Knight Ulrich Von Hutten,

Greetings,

... As to your demand for a complete portrait, as it were, of Thomas More, would that I could execute it with a perfection to match the intensity of your desire! It will be a pleasure, for me as well, to dwell for a space on the contemplation of by far the sweetest friend of all. But in the first place, it is not given to every man to explore all More's gifts. And then I wonder whether he will tolerate being depicted by an indifferent artist; for I think it no less a task to portray More than it would be to portray Alexander the Great or Achilles, and they were no more deserving of immortality than he is. Such a subject requires in short the pencil of an Apelles; but I fear that I am more like Horace's gladiators than Apelles. Nevertheless, I shall try to sketch you an image rather than a full portrait of the whole man,............

Erasmus

Taken from the full letter of Erasmus addressed to Ulrich Von Hutten (1488-1523), the German knight and humanist. Delphi Collected Works of Desiderius Erasmus (Illustrated) (Delphi Series Nine Book 12) . Delphi Classics. Kindle Edition.

Table of Contents

Hermenutics.

Thomas More believed that a diligent and demanding study of liberal arts was necessary to train the soul for virtue: -

Quote; *Without proper training, reason would run riot, and wax over high-hearted and proud and the soul would not fail to fall in rebellion.*

Thomas More

If we were to take a census on which is the most important international artwork that represent man's inhumanity to cause devastation by the stupidity of war, there would be a long tragic list. For me Picassos Guernica is the greatest work which totally represents our socially inclusive desire to wallow in effluence, but he also virtuously attempts to lift the human soul from this destitute poverty. The mad insanity it represents drags everyone down into an immoral pit of depravity, but Picasso with every sinew of his imagination nobly lifts us to a better understanding of our selves. The painting is a dramatic representation of the unnecessary bombing of Guernica, a small Basque Country town in northern Spain. At the invitation of Franco's Nationalist Spanish government Nazi German and Italian warplanes perfected their civilian air bombing techniques Picasso looks to a philosophy of love to say we as human beings do some mad things, but we are also capable of finding divinely inspired goodness together.

In the aftermath Franco, the Germans and the Vatican all with blatant lies tried to cover up their cowardly act and blamed the massacre of the innocents on the Red Republicans. Picasso virtuously depicts Franco as a bewildered minotaur with a fixed gaze of vacant madness amidst a shop floor strewn with body parts.

Franco like all tyrants employed the tactic of the noble lie "loyalty" diverting attention to nationalistic pride, *brothers in arms*, with the jubilant promise of restoring peace and liberty. Whilst with the other hand lashing out anger with shock and awe violence cold calculated inflamed vengeance purposefully intent to intimidate and torment demoralise human minds into mental submission, *"no boss please, please boss restore the peace, anything, anything for peace, we'll do anything you say boss, it is better than the of madness those "Reds" have brought up on us". "Please, please boss we'll do anything you say please give us peace again"* .This is the way all tyrants offer to restore peace and normality which they have done for thousands of years, Picasso asks us to focus our minds not into fighting the tyrants with more violence or living in their fear, but to see through them not to let them bully their way into our psyche, no one can offer you liberty or peace only your "Self".

Link to the Guernica https://www.pablopicasso.org/guernica.jsp

Commendably Picassos dramatic representation fulfils the Hellenistic Greek definition that art was the knowledge of an Idea which had to bestow a benefit for mankind, Only through the love of wisdom could the Hellenistic belief be achieved, only through the finest category of art could the virtue of lady philosophy be revealed, only through this highest art of philosophy can we liberate our soul.

On the same grand scale; Holbein depicted the Thomas More family embracing the universal timeless message that the wisdom of Sophia is overflowing with goodness for the benefit of all mankind through the providence of philosophy.

All that remains of Holbein's original More family portrait is the preparation cartoon, the original composition completed in distemper is now lost and probably destroyed by fire at Kremsier Castle [Czech Republic] in 1752. Holbein on his return to Basel gave this cartoon to Erasmus which was preserved from his belongings.

The full-sized version was completed by Holbein at a time when he was making large disposable scene sets for the Tudor court, because of the unusual size the work it was probably originally displayed as an unframed wall hanging like a tapestry to cover plain walls.

On the cartoon are brown handwritten inscriptions of the ages of the family these are believed to have been added by Nikolaus Kratzer who was tutor and astronomer to the More children he eventually became the official Royal astronomer. There are also German inscriptions by Holbein himself which indicate the modifications to be undertaken for the full-sized version it is unclear if these instructions were given by Erasmus or More.

Above Holbein's original cartoon. [the full sized version is now lost]

Below the life size Nostell Thomas More Family Portrait by an unknown artist.

Devotio Moderna

On the outskirts of Wakefield West Yorkshire there is a small hamlet called Nostell within the parkland stands a grand Palladian mansion house by the same name. The house now owned by the National Trust was built by the fourth Baronette Sir Rowland Winn who married Sussana Henshaw a descendant of Thomas More's favoured daughter Meg [Margaret Roper]. Sussana had two sisters and Rowland was able to buy out their share of the ownership of the portrait, apart from occasional exhibitions it as remained at Nostell since it was shipped from London via the North sea in the 1740's.

The composition is a complete innovation; to represent a family scene in portraiture was almost unknown coupled with the grand scale it makes it unequaled. It also depicts a learned family, commited to the new learning the new modern approach was that children were to be understood with affection. In a world that was dominated by male aggression with little attention given to the thoughts or needs of women here the artist allows the ladies to make the important statements regarding the new learning of affection and understanding. Like all the Tudor paintings by Holbein it is full of allegory and this one is the most Holbeinesque of all his known works, executed with the highest quality of skill it is without doubt the most important piece of Renaissance and Reformation art that was ever undertaken.

The original distemper on cloth was a poor medium used for temporary ephemeral banners and theatrical displays. Whoever commissioned the Nostell portrait had no intention of hiding their light under the table, they wanted to make a grand show piece statement they wanted the superior lasting material of oil on canvas, they had the money, the wall space and most importantly they had a political agenda of promoting the new learning.

There is no firm evidence on how the Henshaws became the owners or who commissioned it or who the artist was. It is most certainly a composition based upon the original portrait Holbein undertook for Thomas More in 1528. The quality and skill is on a par with Holbeins Ambasadors and incredibly twice the size.

From memory I seem to record that Sir Roy Stong dismissed the work as not being good enough for an Holbein particularly because of the poor quality of the hands. It is true Thomas More's hands are painted like fat sausages it could be a correct observation because Erasmus said he had clumsy hands. In contrast to this his son John's you can feel the warm tepid heat. The fur on Thomas More's robe is nothing special, whereas the fur on Ambasadors is so cosy you want to snuggle up to it, but there could equally be good reasons for these possibly poorer details. Then again the velvet on Thomas More's sleeves is perfectly executed, maybe he had on offday when he painted the fur.

More importantly the portrait is a life size representation of the new learning which caused the periods we now call Renaissance and it's subsequent Reformation. I think it is the most important painting in the history of art, long before Picasso this portrait represents the nonviolent struggle for peace, human rights properly including womens rights and those of animals, universal education for all and an end to the class system.

Without the recorded history of the original artist, commisioneer or owner it is shrouded in more mystery than the Turin shroud there is even a novel based upon the suggestions of one gentleman who proposed that the two princes were not killed in the tower of London and the More household surreptitiously rescued them. Which presupposes the highly aspiring family of judges and lawyers have been accomplices to the act of treason. Then again perhaps it is just plausible that the Medieval kings of

England could be renowned for their gracious acts of benevolence and gratuitous mercy?

Before I introduce you to the family allow me to suggest that the portrait is an original Holbein painted in around 1539 composed as a companion piece to the Grand Bible commissioned by Thomas Cromwell and designed by Holbein to be presented to the Nation representing the new learning. Because of Cromwells execution in 1540 the incentive was lost, it remained incomplete, abandoned in some dark back room untill it was liberated by Andre de Loo an avid Holbein collecter who worked has an advisor to Lord Burghley, on his death in 1590 it was sold through auction to one of the More descendants. This work is an important show piece intended for public display done by a skilled artist what other reason could there be for its mysterious origins?

If we consider the points: To produce the portrait it must represent at least six months of dedicated professional time, simply by a process of elimination Holbein is the only artist in Tudor England who had the skill, the philosophical knowledge to make these philosophical statements, he had the contacts who had political motives to commision an art that depicts the new learning, together they would need wall space to make a grand statement including the all important ability to pay the artist.

That's the theory before we put it to the test and visit the family household let me introduce you to the wry old soldier Erasmus, because without Erasmus there is no Holbein. Holbein was just a very skilled jobbing ecclesiastical decorator working on scraps untill he was introduced to Erasmus in 1515. Erasmus gave him the letter of introduction to visit Thomas More in his Chelsea home with the aim he would offer him employment and to Erasmus he returned when he had completed the portrait. Erasmus inspired him to get more philosophy into his art, become a philosophical activist. Erasmus taught him philosophy he became part of Erasmus's revolutionary humanist movement. Erasmus was the child of the Renaissance and the father of the Reformation. Without Erasmus the Renaissance is phony and the Reformation nonexistant. He published the first book in European history devoted entirely to pacifism which he called *Dulce bellum inexpertis* [War is sweet to the inexperienced] written in a style for the general public to grasp. He called for the bible to be written so that everyman could read and understand it which presupposes universal education for all, the new learning of affection. Thus was launched the greatest partnership between client and artist that as ever been in the history of art a mission for universal education.

Holbein produced this show piece of technical brilliance; a huge symbol of nonviolent pacifism, including womens rights, human rights and that universal education would end the class system.

The Christian message is love one another this argument was taken up by Erasmus and his humanist revolution it has always proved controversial and difficult to accept the arguments have persisted, but when they have been won they have always proved to be right thinking.

Erasmus of Rotterdam was just simply "Erasmus". In a world which typified violence and revenge he was a pacifist, who famously said *"he yields to no man"*, he would never soil his hands in anger under any circumstances he was the *new learning*.

Erasmus's early education was through a humanist school known as the Brotherhood of Deventer which originally was patronised by Nicholas of Cusa [Cardinal Cusanus] who was the first European scholar with access to the full Platonic cannon. His teachers practiced *devotio moderna*, the new learning. Cusa introduced to his schools the Platonic concept of the unknowable god which will form a large part of our understanding of the portrait. Although Erasmus records that he hated the school he was given the freedom to absorb the works of the philosophers, this he could chose to do of his own volition and throughout his life he never stopped absorbing philosophy, the Florentine academy was his muse. He became a wonderer with a purpose, finding work to fund his book buying through lecturing, translating, transcribing, publishing, networking seeking contacts who would assist him, give him a bed, he would never make enemies always offering his good Christian fellowship to all. In his later life he settled in Basle, highly influential and wise he was sought as the Delphic oracle by all good men. From Basle he wrote his pacifist booklets which sold in their thousands across Europe. With his humanist conviction he wrote to Kings, Princes, Popes, despots, ambassadors and civil servants appealing for peace and Christian understanding always with his recognisable wry humour. He made it plain his only motive was not who was right or wrong it was the inhumanity against humanity that repelled him. Erasmus and the skill of *Bonae litterae* with swashbuckling swordsmanship blazed a path in pen and ink for history to witness that there was an outstanding man whose heart and soul believed in the true Christian philosophy of nonviolence.

With this simple portrait of Erasmus without further delay let me introduce you to the More family household: -

Above left Margaret Giggs [1508 – 1570] adopted daughter of Sir Thomas More.

Margaret received a classical education in More's household, and married her Greek tutor, Sir John Clements. After Mores execution they both fled onto the continent for safety. She stands with a very serious face next to More's second daughter Elizabeth Dauncey, when compared to the cartoon group not only have, they swopped positions Margaret looks to be a completely different person.

Above right Elizabeth Dauncey Thomas More's second daughter, Notice the book tucked under her arm this is one of three identifiable books. The second one sits on the shelf above her left shoulder.

Above; Sir John More [1451-1530] Judge and lawyer. Judge More believed young Thomas was being influenced by Italian infidels and ordered him to return from Oxford and his Greek studies. He also strongly disproved of Thomas's friendship with Erasmus, he considered him to be shallow, fickle and dangerously overeducated. Obviously as parents go, he is a domineering type who considered Erasmus to be a bad influence on his sons career in the legal profession.

Above right Anne Cresacre [1512-1559]. Daughter of Edward Cresacre of Barmbrough, Doncaster, Yorks. Born 1512; she was betrothed to John More and married to him 1529. At the time of the portrait she was in Thomas Mores care.

The man who needs no introduction he is recognisable from the Frick portrait as Sir Thomas More [1478-1535]. Thomas was a man who called a spade a spade even a dirty spade and he unashamedly published his dirty washing for all to read unequivocally seeking his offensive fights in the public arena. Biographers sometimes seek to excuse his outspoken views as a sign of the times, but the example set by Erasmus demonstrates to us there is no excuse particularly if he desired to be a humanist. More was unashamedly proud to be outspoken which further categorises him has an example of the type of person with a fixed belief that the stronger has the divine right to dominate the weaker. He was educated through a system known as "scholasticism" the old learning of Aristotelian influence despite this to his credit he became a notable humanist scholar. His father's controls contributed to making him extremely narrow minded but well focused for the jobs of law and cases of jurisdiction. For a time, he studied at Charterhouse with Carthusian monks who practiced extreme austerities, which would have further institutionalised and repressed his mind with self-imposed guilt which might explain his underlying obstinate psychological traits with his need for self-harming. To quote Marie Louse von Franz Jungian psychologist and author of Aurora Consurgens "*The scholastic method with a narrow and ridged division of questions and answers in accordance with laws of medieval logic would have caused dammed up emotions, with little outlet*". In my mind if you dam something up, you're trying to exert control, if the dam is not built structurally correct sure enough in time something will give and then there is an uncontrolled destructive burst of energy. The scholastic education was the norm for the elite males of Europe with dammed up emotions ready to burst at the drop of a glove they all must have been stark raving mad, led by the even madder still.

The humanist movement that Erasmus led campaigned against monastic life and scholastic educational trainings which sought to repress the normal natural male thoughts and healthy development which leads to a balanced guilt free minds consequently, Erasmus died suffering with venereal disease but kept a clear head.

More was clearly proud of his achievements and desired to be honoured twice he wrote to Erasmus requesting he publish in haste his self written epitaph, twice Erasmus ignored the request, part of which he states: -

"When he had thus gone through this course of offices or honours, that neither that gracious prince could disallow his doings, nor he was odious to the nobility nor unpleasant to the people, but yet to thieves, murderers and heretics grievous, "

Mores linguistic spade dug deep and sharp into a rich seam of effluence, Erasmus complained that Mores *Responsio ad Lutherum* was so uncouth and splenetic it could give Luther a lesson in vehemence, Mores language is appaulingly vulgar and they both behaved at times like two disgruntled chimney sweeps trying to blacken everyone with their filthy brushes.

If we are understand and learn about our selves from Thomas More there can be no niceties we have to be openly honest with our "Self" excusing his veherment hatred of heretics is deceitful he notoriously stated he would rather incour their animosity. More had a filthy mind and filthy tongue it is shameful to state these comments but he is known to include in his published writtings incitement for mouth urination, he published unashamably seeking a mud slingers fight through foul language and incitement of others to follow his principles making Europe his lavatorial soap box, thankfully most was written in his favoured Latin or a poor broken English, but we would be doing him a great disservice not to take advice from his virtuous preachings of pious moralistic turpitude.

Out of passing interest Erasmus considered the theological argument that was used to support the killing of heretics had been corrupted from the original text: quoting St Paul which says avoid heretics - Latin *"devita"* – avoid, which the theologians corrupt to Latin *de vita* - remove from life.[*In praise of folly*]

The character of Thomas More ticks all the boxes for the perfect image of Aristotle's magnanimous man *par excellence*: *This man hates cowardice, he is arrogant, egocentric and self-opinionated, speaks his mind, thoughtless as to who it offends, seeks honours and gratitude, power, control, self-aggrandisement. His attitude is unduly smug, he has no passionate interest in human interaction, friendship is tepid, friends can be comforted in misfortune, but he does not seek sympathy himself, this is for women and womanish men.*

The magnanimous man is so addicted to his own self-belief that when the doctor advises him that this behaviour is only going to lead to further poor health both physically and mentally, there are two choices he can make carry on or turn around, his dilemma if he turns around, he is a failure to his Aristotelian training. Thomas More was really a man too strong for his own good crying for guidance in a mad wilderness, howling like a chained-up coonhound so head strong that when unleashed cannons head loose straight through the brier and brambles to be found barking up the wrong tree.

Von Franz in her book *Alchemy an introduction to the symbolism and the psychology* [particularly pages 212-230] cites that the Christian religion is one sided in the absence of a feminine goddess, which would provide a mental balance. Typically, a male dominated environment introduces a negative repression of the feminine aspect which can trigger an over whelming influx of the feminine God head. She does not put it into the simple terms which I'm going to do, but by the repression of our inner Sophia she breaks out as over whelming invasion of the unconscious chaos, leading to neurosis which in the medieval period would not have been recognised and even considered normal male behaviour.

The Aristotelian man unfortunately by its very purpose is trained to have no place in his heart for Lady philosophy, More sought the animosity of peaceful nonviolent heretics and I'm afraid I would have been one too, but I have has they had have no animosity only affection and peaceful understanding. Thomas More is our lower self, we are all guilty of doing head strong actions which we regret later when we see the harm, hopefully we learn from them.

Above left, Son, John More [1509- 1547] after the execution of his father along with his sister Elizabeth's husband William Dauncey they were rigorously interrogated. It is said his father's debt and loss of property blighted his life nevertheless, he still fathered eight children to Anne.

Top right, Dress and stature becoming of Henry VIII is Henry Patenson the house jester featured in Shakespeare's Man for all seasons.

"Only a fool can speak the truth and get away with it". [Erasmus In Praise of Folly].

Henry wears symbols of allegiance to the King a crucifix, on his hat there are the red and a white Tudor roses, the red cross of St George and a hawk badge. His hand can be seen firmly griping the sword sheath along with rosary beads around his wrist.

Seated, Cecily Heron Thomas More's third daughter she married Giles Heron who in 1540 was executed for treason and their estates sequestered.

Above; Margarete Roper [1504-1544] Thomas Mores eldest and most favoured daughter affectionately known has Meg. [Ancestor of the Henshaw's]

She wrote to Erasmus in response to his acknowledgement of receipt of the Holbein cartoon. *"There is nothing for which we desire more ardently than to be able to see and speak with our mentor again he whose learned labours have taught us everything we know about liberal arts and the oldest and truest friend to our father"*.

Margaret had a gift for linguistics with an excellent grasp of Latin and Greek which amazingly she never feasted in her father's use of splenetic language.

John Guy in his book *A daughters love* page 64 describes Thomas More's views on her literary ambitions to publish. *"He made it crystal clear that on no account should her character be debased by pandering to what is vain and low, women should know better, their place was to show appropriate modesty"*. According to Guy More was vehemently against any such action advising *"she should rise to true virtue and goods including moral virtue, with his advice he considered she had to avoid pride and lead an innocent life only this way could she face death without dread"*. Bravely she defied the Demon Death and the threats of his partner and took the risk of upsetting the sundry places of Christendom. With her skills of translation she published her version of Erasmus's *Precatio dominicai* which she titled *A Devout Treatise upon the Pater Noster*, written by a woman in support for other women, in doing so she got herself into serious trouble with the league for heresies and felt her father's wrath, her book was needlessly withdrawn….. Such was her respect and devotion to the ideals of Erasmus.

[John Guy ditto page 149]

 Above left the messenger Johanes heresius the name is thought to be a Latin derivative of Thomas Mores secretary John Harris who collated Mores works after his death. He is not featured on the original cartoon; this suggests the introduction fulfils a special purpose.

Seated Alice More the second wife of Thomas More with whom there were no children. Erasmus records after the death of his first wife "*He would not endure to live long a widower, although his friends counselled otherwise. Within a few months of his wife's death he married a widow, more for the care of the household than for his pleasure, as she was not precisely beautiful nor, as he jokingly says himself, a girl, but a keen and watchful housewife; with whom he yet lives as pleasantly and agreeably as if she were a most charming young girl. Hardly any husband gets so much obedience from his wife by stern orders as he does by jests and cajolery. How could he fail to do so, after having induced a woman on the verge of old age, also by no means a docile character, and lastly most attentive to her business, to learn to play the cittern, the lute, the monochord and the recorders, and perform a daily prescribed exercise in this at her husband's wish".*

[Quoted from Erasmus, Desiderius. Delphi Collected Works of Desiderius Erasmus (Illustrated). Delphi Classics. Kindle Edition.

Beneath her chair is a chained monkey if this was a dog it would represent a sign of fidelity, but here Alice is adorned in the refinements of gold.

Commenting in the same letter to Ulrich Von Hutten Erasmus made the following statement regarding Thomas Mores first wife Jane Colt; the mother of his four children.

Still, he married a girl, as yet very young, of good family, but still untrained — she had always lived in the country with her parents and sisters — so that he could better fashion her to his own ways. He had her taught literature and made her skilled in all kinds of music; and he had really almost made her such as he would have cared to spend all his life with, had not an untimely death carried her off while still a girl.

On education Thomas More appears to take his advice from the guidelines of Aristotle Politics book VIII in which there are four arts which children are to be taught, reading, gymnastic exercises, music the fourth some painting. Of which music is considered particularly important for purpose of instructing and purifying the soul the harmonies of which are a moral education to please the ear, and sooth the mind as the art of a physician producing harmonies that are so strong as to overpower the soul.

An Unknown Artist.

There are two copies of the Nostell composition one at Chelsea Old Town Hall and the other at East Hendred Oxfordshire. They are clearly later copies of the Nostell composition and poorly executed, thus they can be dismissed from this exercise particularly because they have no worthwhile artistic merit.

The composition to consider is a montage now belonging to the National portrait gallery by Rowland Lockey 1593 or possibly later. [see page 23]

Thomas More and his immediate family are represented in montage with their descendants of the period who probably commissioned Lockey to produce this version.

Featured on the portrait are Thomas More II and his wife who were Catholic recusants, Thomas supported a secret printing press run by English Jesuits. He was released from prison in 1586, for his observance in the Catholic faith he continued to be issued fines until his death in 1606.

The composition is an highly skilled montage made to order by an accomplished hand but lacks any original artistic inspiration and is purely a good generative copy of the individuals without Nostell's political or philosophical meaning. For example Margaret Roper holds the third book which we will examine here the book is blank like his subjects they resemble expressionless cardboard cut outs.

Therefore, Lockey and the family do not see any importance to the political philosophy of the Nostell composition, the symbolism is completely meaningless, all parties are oblivious to the religious implications. We can say categorically a good Catholic family does not see any inspirational merit in the new learning that the three pagan books named on the Nostell composition represent.

Above Lockey circa 1593 Thomas More and his descendants.

However Lockey is undoubtably using the Nostell composition to copy from because of the inclusion of the flowers for example, which are not part of the Holbein cartoon. Additionally the hand movements of Cilcey are the exact same and she does not hold her rosary beads which are the traditional symbol of Christian piety.

The iris is a symbol of virtue, hope and prosperity it was used for Elizabeths rainbow portrait of the same period. To my mind on the Nostell version the distance the two iris vases are apart with an apple on the one in the righthand window signifies a long and fruitful prosperity but we need to stress all these allegorical symbols can be subjective and need concrete information.

It is a strong possibility that Lockey is copying his montage from the Nostell composition at the bequest of the More family featured and not the original distemper one. Take for example Judge More's facial expression which lacks the character of the Nostell one which is identical to the original Holbein Windsor castle sketch. Infact all the original casting of faces are inferior to the Nostell version which are all very closely matched to the Windsor Castle sketches.

An important point to consider is that by using the Nostell version he would not have needed the Holbein sketches now stored in Windsor Castle which would probably have not been available to him had he even known about them.

This presupposes the Nostell version is older than 1593 and we can safely deduct that prior to 1593 there was only two versions in existance. The Nostell and the original distemper which Lockey did not use or need.

The reason that the More family commisioned Lockey is that he was an excellent copiest. An educated guess is that the family have seen the Nostell version and requested their montage. Why 1593? Around 1590 an auction was held in London on behalf of the deceased Andries de Loo an avid collector of Holbeins work recorded by the art historian Van Mander. Van Mander also records that a member of the More family owned a very large life sized water colour on canvas of Thomas More and his family which was bought by a member of the More family from Andrie de Loo's collection. It becomes an obvious assumption that one section of the family have seen the Nostell version belonging to another and asked Lockey to make them a commemorative version.

Andries de Loo was an active advisor to Lord Burghley on the religious conflicts in the Netherlands and would have had opportunities to seek out lost works of Holbein in the Royal court. With a name like "de Loo" he is almost certainly of Huguenot desent and working for Lord Burghley he would not have been a Catholic sympathiser which is why he has an interest in Holbein.

Van Mander recorded notable artwork of the period; his book titled Schilderboek was first published in 1604. For the Andries de Loo record he is reporting from a second-hand report and therefore it is probable it is not without error. His advisor refers to a *very large canvas in water colour* but is he referring to the distemper composition or the Nostell oil on canvas. The suggestion is strongly towards the Nostell version because of the above conclusions and what follows?

Lord Arundel cleared Holbein's workshop in 1547 and his family owned the original distemper portrait, their records show this was sold in 1673, but was listed on an inventory dated 1641. Bearing in mind Thomas More's property was all sequestered on his death in 1535. It seems implausible that if the More family had somehow managed to take reposition would they have resold it to Lord Arundel particularly considering they had the money to pay Lockey to produce their montage?

Adding also the Nostell version was most certainly not commissioned by a Catholic family, just on consideration of the iris flowers alone representing *"providence"* which is an entirely different theology to faith and belief. And we have not yet considered the political messages of the books.

The rainbow goddess Iris in her role as the messenger of the gods brings providence. Iris is the daughter of "wonder" according to Socrates this is the cause of the philosophers passion to "wonder", therefore, to wonder - to reason is to reject faith and belief by beginning the quest to search for the true cause of his passion "wonder" then becomes providential. [Theaetetus 155d]

Incidentally, in passing another Platonic term which means the same as providence is "Eros".

It can be deducted from the Van Mander record that a section of the More family bought a More family portrait belonging to Andries de Loo and passed it down the inheritance line till it reached Sussanna's mother which appears to be the case.

Recording in 1731 George Vertue remembers seeing the Nostell portrait in 1723 at Well Hall Eltham Kent, home of the Roper's then again in 1726 and finally at Soho Square in 1731 in the ownership of Rowland Winn of Nostell. He records that the Roper family bought it from a sale of Andries de Loo's estate.

Notes:

The information referring to the records of Vertue, Van Mander are from Lesley Lewis: *The Thomas More family group Portraits after Holbein.*

With this conclusion I am suggesting Holbein and Cromwell had the original distemper version delivered to his workshop for a template to design the Nostell composition, there it remained till discovered by Lord Arundel clearing out the old workshop. Distemper is an ephemeral medium, Cromwell and Holbein would have wanted something less perishable, the size wood of panels which were used for the

Ambassadors may have been prohibitive it makes sense to use the relatively technically advanced medium of oil on canvas.

The Nostell composition is the perfect way in the period to symbolise the new learning. Cromwell was on a mission of social change introducing the "new learning" concept of providence which is not fully appreciated by his historians particularly if they have been schooled in faith and belief. Thomas More represented the strongest symbol of the old order, Cromwell functioned as the new order which was that espoused by Erasmus; universal education. There is so much false gossip about Cromwell that we must ignore this and stick to his "function" what was he trying to achieve? He was re-educating England in the new learning which is what we are aiming to explore shortly. Holbein studied with Erasmus and understands the new learning; Cardinal Wolsey was a great admirer of Erasmus; Cromwell was trained by Wolsey is this the connection? Thomas More as already stated is a completely narrow minded black and white thinker and because of his exemplary erudite scholastic training he cannot possibly understand the new learning in short, his mental ability does not go there. Holbein is the trusted court artist working directly to secretary Cromwell amongst his output was a woodcut for the Coverdale bible sanctioned by Henry and Cromwell. Cromwell wanted a Grand Bible that the common man could read and understand therefore his dream, his desire is education for all a true Utopia. An end of the class system, modern day people frown upon the Indian class system of untouchables, this Tudor period is on a par. Cromwell had less than six years of power and if he had been given another the English social and education system would have changed dramatically far superior to the continental medieval scholastic mentality, unfortunately the ignorance of his scholastic foes brought him down. The cause of his execution was the marriage of Henry to Anne of Cleves whose father was a known Erasmian sympathiser. The evidence is that Cromwell was firmly pushing for the reforms that Erasmus advocated, he took a step-in haste.

Where was the justice, one of the chief aims of Plato's Republic is how to recognise the unjust man from the just man? The unjust man is a perfectionist in injustice so perfect everyone believes he is just. The just man never hurts anyone, never does any harm never even incites anyone to violence but everyone believes he is corrupt and unjust and want to punish him abuse him and eventually after every humiliation they make an exhibition of him by mounting him on a pole like they do with crows and weasels.

The medieval period of the Renaissance was under the control of an oppressive fascist regime; Holbein spent at least ten years before arriving in England working with Erasmus and his underground resistance network. Additionally, in contrast Luther who was also scholastically educated his vociferous writings infected Europe with a plague of uncontrolled war. Cromwell was steering a very different ship through the storm one of restoring Sophia at the helm of state. Secretary of state Cromwell was ambitiously and unambiguously delivering the message that education is for all, the new messenger delivering the new learning. In my mind to be commended amongst the bravest of all men to have ever lived; living in a pit of savage dogs he was clearly planning to avoid violence wherever possible in a dark mad age of predatory oppression.

I found this quote regarding Queen Elizabeth I at the helm it could easily be referring to Cromwell who built the sailing ship.

Who confounded the Projects, and destroy'd the Power

that threaten'd to oppress the Liberties of Europe;

took off the Yoke of Ecclesiastical Tyranny;

restor'd Religion from the Corruptions of Popery;

and by a wise, moderate, and a popular Government,

gave Wealth, Security, and Respect to England. [From the Elysian field of Stowe]

The three philosophical books featured on the Nostell composition were the favourites of Elizabeth and for a time I thought with the iris connection this was a reference to Elizabeth, but the evidence I am sure points to the way I am leading you.

Above a section from Holbein's woodcut for the Coverdale bible 1535 Henry with sword firmly grasped in his right hand a symbol of the bible being his idea.

From this woodcut the sword became a symbol of the Protestant bible, notice Henry Patenson his left hand grasps the scabbard of the sword not the hilt are Cromwell and Holbein having a private jest with Henry VIII who would have enjoyed the humour. Henry remained a Catholic and here Henry Patenson can be seen wearing the rosery beads around his wrist. The hawk and the hen symbolise a topsy-turvy world, but a "hawk" on his hat must mean calm, stability and providence. This form of reasoning could point to the Nostell portrait being Elizabethan but Lockey's ignorance of the new learning demonstrates there is no one left capable of understanding let alone creating the political messages contained in the Nostell composition. Additionally, Lockey was apprenticed to Nicholas Hilliard they are part of the network of Elizabethan Royal court painters, if the Nostell masterpiece was done in the Elizabethan period a professional show piece like this with the known contacts would have been recorded and not gone unnoticed. By this I mean the artist or commissioner is making a bold political statement they are advertising their ideals not hiding them covertly. The intellect on the magnitude of the Nostell portrait is absent in the Lockey montage and any other Elizabethan art of the period.

The political messages of the Nostell composition are older than the Elizabethans remit and there is no one who had the invention to use them it is if the new learning arrived from outer space and then vanished.

To sum up so far, I have introduced you to Plato and Socrates who are the major influences on Erasmus and his Reformation movement, the next step is to continue with the history of the portraits by discussing the Windsor Castle sketches created by Holbein.

Holbein sketches from the Windsor Castle archive Judge More, followed by Lady Barkley below her Mother Iak.

The labelling of Windsor Castle sketches of Lady Barkley and Mother lak was made from the information in the *great booke* compiled by Sir John Cheke a Greek scholar and secretary to King Edward (1514-1557). Cheke began his career at court under the patronage of Anne Boleyn, in 1544 he became tutor to Edward VI. He would have known visually most of Holbein's sitters he was on personal terms with most, it seems inconceivable that he would get the identification for those associated with the courts of Anne Boleyn and Edward wrong.

Cheke's *great booke* belonged to the Earl of Arundel after clearing Holbein's workshop [1547] at this stage none of the sketches where labelled up until much later.

In 1945 K. T. Parker catalogued Holbein's sixty-four sketches held in Windsor castle finding nine errors against the eighteenth-century labelling compiled by using Cheke's inscriptions.

Researchers Bendor Grosvenor and David Starkey recently narrowed this down to just two Lady Barkley and Mother lak the sitters for the Nostell composition.

[see link: - https://www.arthistorynews.com/articles/894_Anne_Boleyn_regains_her_head]

They are also suggesting Mother lak could be the sitter to the famous East Harling Anne Lovell squirrel and the starling portrait as the Latin for starling is sternus meaning nurse and the squirrel is an appropriate pet for a child.

Lady Barkley does look extremely like Elizabeth Dauncey on both the original cartoon and Nostell portrait and must be assumed to be wrongly labelled, however Margret Giggs on the cartoon is completely different including dress and pose. This suggest Chekes labelling is correct for Mother lak and Holbien needed a fresh sitter with different facial expressions for a new composition and chose Mother lak. Without the evidence of the Nostell portrait she would always be known to this day as Mother lak and probably the sitter to the squirrel and starling.

The Mother lak sketch was in Lord Arundels collection from 1547 changing hands several times till it became part of the official Royal collection at Windsor. To compose the Nostell portrait somewhere along the lines an unknown commisioner, who had considerable wealth, political motive and wall space needed to collaborate out of the blue with an unknown exceptional artist with no other recorded works but with considerable professional skill, political and philosophical knowledge they then needed access to Lord Arundels collection. Unless these unknown people with a strong political agenda chose the Mother lak drawing because they liked the way she was plainly dressed or for some other random reason they needed permission from Lord Arundel and co. This is a private potentially Royalist collection no one would have had open access to take them away and use them covertly in a studio to paint a scene representing iconic supremacy of Catholicism. Considering the hostilities placed upon Elizabeth by the Pope for heracies, is anyone going to knock on Lord Arundels door and ask politely if they can borrow them?

Conclusion to produce the Nostell composition no owners or artists have used the Holbein sketches to create the Nostell More family portrait other than Holbein who died in 1543. This same artist used the original distemper as a template and made alterations to suit the political requirements of the time.

Mother Iak would have nused Edward from his birth in 1537 and be known to the Royal court possibly earlier.

Lady Barkley was a maid to Anne Boleyn, Holbein could have known her prior to 1528 and used her image for the sketch in the absence of Elizabeth?

This suggests the timeline for the Nostell composition is between 1535-1543. 1538 must be excluded on account of Holbeins commitments abroad. 1540-1543 must also be dismissed as Holbein was no longer the favoured artist following Cromwells execution. Any date prior to Thomas More's execution must also be dismissed because of the story paralleled in the second book which we will discuss later.

A complete guess is that Lord Arundel recovered the original distemper version from Holbeins workshop, that it had been taken there for Holbein and Cromwell to discuss the composition layout for a new version which was going to be presented to the Nation as a propaganda companion piece to the Great Bible. With Cromwells execution this was aborted and perhaps left uncomplete. This was some how discovered by Andres de Loo whilst working for Lord Burghley and became a More family heirloom after the auction of his estate.

Notes

For detailed information on the Windsor Castle sketches

https://www.rct.uk/collection/search#/page/1

The history of the ownership of the sketches produced by Holbein for Henry VIII: -

Henry VIII; Edward VI, 1547; Henry FitzAlan, 12th Earl of Arundel; by whom bequeathed to John, Lord Lumley, 1580; by whom probably bequeathed to Henry, Prince of Wales, 1609, and thus inherited by Prince Charles (later Charles I), 1612; by whom exchanged with Philip Herbert, 4th Earl of Pembroke, 1627/8; by whom given to Thomas Howard, 14th Earl of Arundel; acquired by Charles II by 1675.

In 1980 the canvas of the Nostell composition was carbon dated to 1520 or earlier.

The art historian Ellis Waterhouse discussed the Lockey attribution in a letter in the Burlington Magazine in 1957, mentioning the Nostell composition at an Holbein attribution in the RA exhibition, said, "I …… believe the picture is better left out of any consideration of the Lockey canon".

Sir Roy Strong, former director of the National Portrait Gallery, commenting on the original distemper noted the *"its destruction means we lost the greatest single visual artefact to epitomize the aims and ideals of the early Renaissance in England"* and calls the composition *"arguably the greatest and most innovative work of Holbein's English period"* and *"the earliest conversation piece in English painting".*

He also dismissed any suggestion that the Nostell painting was a Holbein, but his comments are spot on it is *"the greatest single visual artefact to epitomize the aims and ideals of the early Renaissance in England".* Certainly, it epitomises the new learning more than he could have imagined.

Derek Wilson [the author of *Hans Holbein portrait of an unknown man*] explains Holbeins use of diagonals on the Ambasadors and similar examples can be found on the Nostell composition. He states he has seen every Holbein and discussed them with experts and sees no reason why the Nostell picture is not given to Holbein. His view is there is no other known artist capable.

Timeline

July 23rd, 1519 Erasmus wrote humanist friend Ulrich Von Hutten with an almost clinical dossier on the character of Thomas More. Hutten was gauging an insight to Mores psychological character, possibly he was planning a strategy for potential meetings, the letter is carefully worded and guarded, but it is more than a few personal advisory tips and a friendly jovial observation there is a serious business tone to It. We cannot analyse the whole letter, but there are key points which can help our understanding into the psyche of Thomas More, Erasmus begins: -

But in the first place, it is not given to every man to explore all More's gifts. And then I wonder whether he will tolerate being depicted by an indifferent artist; for I think it no less a task to portray More than it would be to portray Alexander the Great or Achilles, and they were no more deserving of immortality than he is. Such a subject requires in short, the pencil of an Apelles; but I fear that I am more like Horace's gladiators than Apelles. Nevertheless, I shall try to sketch you an image rather than a full portrait of the whole man.

Without doubt Holbein was destined to become the new Apelles.

An important event of 1515 was that Holbein the son of a journeyman ecclesiastical artist and destined to follow his footsteps was approached to personalise the margins of a newly published work called *Encomium Moriae*, (In praise of Folly). On completion Erasmus was presented this book in appreciation by an ardent admirer, it now included a series of pencil caricatures. The drawings perfectly complement Erasmus's satirical wit as if the two men had been born with identical humour and were equally prepared to take risks with its ambiguity for delivering poignant truths. The humanist movement centred around Erasmus enabled Holbein to develop the skills for the Hellenistic understanding of art in that art must be a benefit to mankind by representing wisdom.

By 1522 with their partnership well established the new Apelles was painting and drawing the philosopher on a regular basis, Erasmus would then send the portraits as token of friendship to his contacts in Europe. One of these portraits now hangs in the National Gallery; London, if you ever view it you will gradually notice the hands, Holbein paints hands that talk, Erasmus's are black with ink, Erasmus was a warrior with a quill for a sword, there can be no doubt that Holbein was encouraged to apply philosophy in his art from the wisest man in the all of Christendom who's hands rest delicately on *Novum instrumentum* his translation of the New Testament.

The envoy of Erasmus: Holbein arrived in London in late 1526 with a letter of introduction address to Thomas More in the hope that he or his contacts would offer him lucrative commissions?

After completing a variety commissions including the now famous Frick portrait of Thomas More, he returned to Basel in mid-1528 with the explanation he had to sort out his personal estate and master guild licences. He took this opportunity with his hard-earned cash to purchase a house which provided for the future security of his family.

Later that year he was back in London, then by August 1529 he had returned to Basel; Erasmus corresponded to Margarete Roper admiring the cartoon of the completed life-sized portrait of the family which Holbein had brought him.

[This chronology was taken from Derek Wilson; *Hans Holbein portrait of an unknown man*]

This suggests because of Erasmus's letter in his second stay he must have completed the original distemper family portrait. More was appointed chancellor in 1529 and he made this celebratory jubilant comment to Erasmus, … *"I have a driving ambition to be as hateful as anyone can possibly be towards this absolutely loathsome breed of men "*.

Obviously, he was seeking approval, which was not forthcoming.

There are people who opinion that Thomas More did not preside over man burning, if we disregard this argument; he was nevertheless inciting violence, banning books, instigating armed raids into the Steelyard, overturning houses for heretical books and prepared to arrest and torture anyone caught with them. Which to my mind is the type of loathsome controlling activities the gestapo used; with inexcusable violence particularly when we can define heretics in this instance to be simple nonviolent peaceful men who wanted to read the bible in English in order to gain a deeper personal spiritual understanding of Christianity.

Further on condemning heretics he wrote "*I find that breed of men absolutely loathsome, so much so that unless they regain their senses, I want to be as hateful to them as anyone can be.*"

Whilst in London Holbein made frequent visits to his clients working in the Steelyard, he would have been fully aware of Thomas Mores notorious brown shirt activities. The intense hostilities caused by Thomas More must have been at least equal to our present day understanding of Nazi Germany. Holbein with his moral conviction would have not wanted to overstay his welcome but with his skill and being coached by Erasmus rest assured Apelles is there for a reason and their going to stitch him up in the most subtle of ways.

There are volumes of More's correspondence with his consistent aggressive incitement for violence and, regardless of when or who wrote it is immoral, vile and fascist which cannot be condoned, but the root cause is the scholastic education he received.

[The vengeful quotes by Thomas More can be found in: *A daughters love* John Guy pages 163,197 -8].

More used his new powers to lead his personal vendetta for state sponsored persecution of his heretics. This is a world where leaders solve their problems with violence, to quote More, "*history proves that violence is always necessary to restrain the great outrages committed against the peace and quiet of the people in the sundry places of Christendom by heretics…. For this reason, many sore punishments had been devised for them and especially fire"*. The quote is from his *A Dialogue Concerning Heresies* where he lectures a messenger in his private study on Christian theology. During his chancellorship over one hundred books would be added to the list of heretical works including Tyndale's New Testament, which is virtually the same as the popular authorised King James bible we have today, ironically Tyndale was translating from the one written by Erasmus. The violent punishment methods to oppress his victims have been tried and tested by tyrants for thousands of years and are still commonly used today, *fire* as many disguises which Picasso represented in the Guernica. The pagan philosopher Socrates, who was a notable early pacifist, exposes the use of violence in many interesting ways this is just one simple illustration: -

The function of coolness is not to heat, but it's opposite, the function of wetting does not cause dryness, but the opposite, therefore harming does not cause goodness, but the opposite then it is not the function of a just man to harm anyone at any time. [Rep 335d-e]

To quote Erasmus: -

"Farther, they make as many partitions and divisions in hell and purgatory and describe as many different sorts and degrees of punishment as if they were very well acquainted with the soil and situation of those infernal regions". [Judge Folly – *In Praise of Folly*]

When Erasmus published his revised New Testament in the comments, he was calling for the bible to be translated into the different languages so that ordinary people could read and understand which if you follow his reasoning, he means universal education. This is because he was not schooled has a scholastic and was freely allowed to read the new thinking of Plato.

During 1530's the reformist MP Thomas Cromwell became increasingly influential in the Royal Court and by 1532, he was Henry's chief advisor.

Coincidentally Holbein returned to England after talking to his German associate Simon Grynaeus who had just spent three months in Henry's

Royal court, on his advice that political scene was changing it was now safe for a return. [More was losing favour and he would soon be out]. Holbein throughout these three years lived of casual scraps in Basel; soon he was back in England again earning the mega bucks.

Reviewing Holbein's movements, it would appear he initially did a reconnaissance, reported back to Erasmus, discussed the plan, returned to London completed the group family portrait in distemper, accomplished the deed and got out quickly before More rumbled the sting. Whatever was included within the portrait composition we will never know? Erasmus on the receipt of the preserved cartoon given to him by Holbein makes this innocent reply to Margaret Roper which suggests a tone of bubbling superior satisfaction.

The reply from Erasmus reads; *I'm scarcely able to express in words, my dear Margaret Roper, ornament of Britain, the pleasure I felt in my heart when the painter Holbein depicted for me your entire family like this, so skillfully that even if I'd been present among you, I could hardly have seen you all more clearly. How often I've found myself privately wishing that just once more before I die, I could have the pleasure of seeing that little circle of friends that is so dear to me and whom I owe a good part of my fame and reputation.*

Margaret replied that she missed her mentor who had taught her all she knew of *liberal arts*.

History makes us nostalgic, it makes these events seam remote, sometimes innocently quaint we long for those good old days the quiet sundry lanes of Christendom with peace and solitude good will to all men, don't be fooled the humanist movement which Erasmus was orchestrating was on a par with the war time Spanish and French resistance movements. He lived in a harsh world where there was no press coverage, no sentiment or toleration for heretics a comment which was frequently aimed at Erasmus. Humanists who had the revolutionary views of Erasmus walked the razors edge; they could be dragged in by the inquisition for heresies at any time and their memory besmirched and obliterated. All manner of fire and brimstone was used to suppress the advancing changes being brought through the new humanist learning, cartwheel crucifixion, burning alive, the women even buried alive, threats of open genocide uncivilised madness plagued Europe apparently under the divine approval of Jesus Christ. Unfortunately, the works of Erasmus ignited the anger of Luther against the Catholic Pope and because Erasmus was not prepared to be involved with any form of anger, he was caught between two raging fires. The Lutheran movement resulted in anger and the counter Reformation replied with anger, anger plagued Europe. The scholastic shock and awe brutality including the many sore punishments especially fire was a contagious plague that raged with universal infection for all. The Lutherans and the Hapsburgs slugged it out together in the darkness like two blind tyrannical dinosaurs each sweeping swathe of the tail left power vacuums for others to envelope and encourage the flames.

In contrast the humanist movement of Erasmus employed a nonviolent resistance in the form of subtle mockery, and he left a legacy for us to read. A thousand years of state-controlled tyranny was being steadily undermined, the language, the rituals and customs, the politics, the educational system, that dominated Latin Medieval Europe through the ruling Catholic hierarchy was beginning to collapse with the missile of ridicule. It all centred on the skills of one man with a pen and a dry sense of humour.

Now I have painted the picture of madness, next I wanted to return to the Hutten quote and draw your attention to the suggestion of the portrayal of Alexander the Great linked with Thomas More. Erasmus stops short of calling him a tyrant like Alexander but nevertheless by subtle implication he does.

But in the first place, it is not given to every man to explore all More's gifts. And then I wonder whether he will tolerate being depicted by an indifferent artist; for I think it no less a task to portray More than it would be to portray Alexander the Great or Achilles, and they were no more deserving of immortality than he is. Such a subject requires in short, the pencil of an Apelles; but I fear that I am more like Horace's gladiators than Apelles. Nevertheless, I shall try to sketch you an image rather than a full portrait of the whole man.

By doing this Erasmus avoids the necessity to call Thomas More a blood thirsty tyrant with ambitions equal to Alexander the Great, but nevertheless he implants the seeds along with his similar view of Tudor Britain. By aggregating this statement with the one below it can be determined that Erasmus conceives Thomas More to have a tyrannical nature: -

"For women generally, even for his wife, he has nothing but jests and merriment. You could say he was a second Democritus, or better, that Pythagorean philosopher who saunters through the marketplace with a tranquil mind gazing on the uproar of buyers and sellers. None is less guided by the opinion of the herd, but again none is less remote from the common feelings of humanity".

To pull this together firstly Erasmus uses a typical Socratic ploy; which means we are to add *"he has no feelings for humanity* to the comment on *"for women generally, even for his wife"*.

Then he likens Thomas More to Democritus which he did in his previously mentioned work called *In Praise of Folly,* but here he says a better description of him is, *an unnamed philosopher with little feelings for humanity.* Erasmus is inferring More is self-opinionated like Alexander who was Educated by Aristotle and consequently believed he was divinely authorised to rule the world, but who is the unnamed philosopher? Hutten would recognise the unnamed philosopher to be the sophist Isocrates who suffered from a speech impediment and never actually gave speeches but made phenomenal amounts of money from the education of his students. He encouraged them to learn human behavioural traits by wandering and observing crowds in the streets and markets. Additionally, Isocrates most definitely would not follow the herd he is most defiantly a lead bull with a minotaur mentality. His academy was established to teach politicians the art of rhetoric and oratory, the professional powers of speech and good language which in turn is applied to convince or persuade the human herd to any given argument. He formed the first academy of rhetoric in the Lyceum which Aristotle later became the patron which in turn paved the development of the scholastic schools. The pupils are taught to present and argue in favour of the king or ruler regardless of the opinion being right or wrong the objective of the game is to settle it in favour of their pay master. In practice if you get two sophists arguing together it leads to war, unnecessary war because the best trained sophist like fighting cocks do not know when to stop arguing over what is after all only ephemeral opinion. Fundamentally Isocrates is the founding father of Western education systems his ideology is still employed to tutor the civil leaders of education, politics, religion, laws, military etc.

Isocratic sophists solve their problems with violence, they punish disobediences and excel at manipulate crowds, [Rep 492d] like bestial animals must fight for the right rule of the harem by using brute force [Rep 411d-e]. Isocratic rhetoric follows the trends of fashion always selling the survival of the fittest mentality cunningly dressed in emperor's new clothes which we still today unknowingly buy into.

Biographers of Thomas More commonly assert he was renowned for his early prowess of oratory and rhetorical excellence used to support civic philosophy. The description applies to Isocrates who opinions that through his rhetorical training a person will become good who learns to speak eloquently, then accordingly when the speech becomes accurate the words, he speaks are equally representations of truth. We all opinion that persons who speaks well must know what they are talking about, but is it really any sign of virtue? Below is our first Isocrates quote from his Antidosis a mock trial set in response to the trial of Socrates in Plato's Apology.

"To speak well is taken as the surest index of a sound understanding which is true and lawful and just as is the outward image of a good soul". [Antidosis 255]

Erasmus adds a further Isocratic description of More in his lesser known work called Ciceronianus: -

"A most fortunate genius. I confess there is nothing he could not have accomplished if he had devoted himself wholly to letters. But in his boyhood scarcely a trace of the better literature had crossed into England. Then the authority of his parents compelled him to learn English Law, the farthest possible from literature; next he was exercised in pleading cases, then called to the duties of the state. With difficulty he could at odd hours turn his attention to the study of oratory. Finally, he was dragged into Court and immersed in the business of the King and the Kingdom where he could love study but not cultivate it. Though the style he gained tended rather to Isocratic rhythm and logical subtlety than to the outpouring river of Ciceronian eloquence, yet he is not inferior at all in culture to Cicero. Further more, you recognize a poet even in his prose for in his youth he spent much time in writing poetry".

The words to this paragraph must be carefully unpacked; firstly, note he says the better literature scarcely a trace had crossed into England and secondly the law studies he gained where Isocratic in rhythm which were as far as possible from this literature. Erasmus refers to Devotio Moderna the new learning which the Nostell portrait reflects. He says the English law system is based upon Isocratic principles. He also refers to Thomas Mores abilities to write poetry, which further suggest More is trained has an Isocratic rhetorician.

Together these statements provide the following evidence: firstly, we can confirm the courts and the English justice system is based upon Isocratic rhetoric that to speak well is to speak the truth in which More was trained. Secondly, we can deduct that Thomas More has been educated in a way that is as far removed from Devotio Moderna, meaning the new learning was beyond his grasp. [Rep 587e].

Thirdly Erasmus likens Thomas More to Isocrates and Democritus but because of his scholastic education we can infer by implication he also considers him Aristotelian trained. To Erasmus these three are the biggest state sponsored educators of tyrants the world has ever known including the power-driven madness of it all.

A philosopher is a lover of Sophia; however, this trio of bandits are deeply misogamist and femininity does not even enter their dogmas, its womanish therefore strictly speaking their doctoring is philodoxes, lovers of their own opinions and as such do not earn the right to be listed amongst philosophers.

There are at least two occasions when Erasmus calls Thomas More a young Democritus here then is a good stage to quickly examine what he infers by this.

Democritus was an early Greek researcher in the liberal arts he wrote extensively on these sciences, but his works have not survived they are only extant in other people's work in the form of loose short fragmented quotes.

He is known as the laughing philosopher more correctly a scoffer and he is greatly admired by modern science for his statements regarding atoms.

The theory he proposed was that all that exists are "atoms and emptyness", which is considered to be very enlightened for the period giving rise to the modern physical understanding of atoms. He further postulates that nothing stays the same because the atoms are all colliding, gyrating, intertwing, rebounding which our senses perceive through an infinate variety of changing shapes and disguises.

Here's the twist, there is a strangly worded fragment [B 125] *"Poor thought, do you take your warrants from us and then over-throw us? Our over throw is your down fall"*.

With this bizarre fragment we have to imagine he is speaking on behalf of his all important "atoms" and the atoms are issuing a threat to our "thought" namely our intellect meaning his atoms have the right to invade our personal thought to think freely, the audacity! He infers his atoms are the dominating force, the rulers of our world which is why it changes and if we don't succumb to this appreciation these atom gods will pull the rug from under our feet. These atoms gods move around in an indiscriminate way knowing the way they move is a matter of conjecture which is why he is so hooked on opinion. Thus Democritus holds that the mind attains knowledge through the senses and sense experience gained by observation of atoms is all there is.

We can gather through his fastidious studies Democritus is obsessed with understanding the physical phenomal world of constant change, he likens the atoms to pebbles on a beach, pebbles naturally congregate in clusters, therefore like attracts like.

He infers our physical world is governed by an indiscriminate theory of ruling atoms, which he then transposes with the visual example of pebbles being washed and buffeted around the shore line. He believes that this massing together holds a powerful effect.

Taking the example of pebbles at a practical level it's easy to see he is talking of herd mentality, cattle spooked in a field for no apparent reason, they gather by safety of numbers with the weaker ones being naturally picked off by predators. This congregating is done for individual survival but more importantly survival of species. A multitude of soldiers gathered together is a powerful force and perfect example of this herd mentality.

Democritus considers its utterly foolish to think that two or more things might ever become one and that from nothing only comes nothing.

Plato's philosophy considers the physical world of opinions is always changing his philosophy ultimately resides in the metaphysical world of the eternal unchangeable truths of wisdom, truth, beauty and justice in which everything can only be "One" because if there were two or more "ones" which one would be the truest "one" it would come down to a choice of opinion. The metaphysical does not exist if it did it would have to be a subject of opinion and so the metaphysical world in Platonism becomes entirely nothingness "Via Negativa" that which you can say nothing about, but crazily this nothingness created our physical world of opinion. To put this simply all there "is" is a pure indescribable intellect for which we and our world are a manifestation of. If this seems inexplicable that is exactly right we can only say that we are part of it and what it is not.

Here are a few other snippits of Democritus vagueness which if you can take time to consider when put into practice what would be the the results of his advice.

A courageous man is not only one who conquers his enemies but also one who is superior to pleasures, some men rule cities and are slaves to women. [B 214]

It is not refraining from injustice which is good, but not even wanting it. [B 62]

Only those who hate injustice are loved by the gods [B 217]

It is better for fools to be ruled than to rule. [B 75]

Justice is doing what should be done, injustice not doing what should be done but turning away from it. [B 256]

One should kill at any cost all which offend against justice; and anyone who does this will in every society have a greater share of contentment and justice and boldness and property. [B 258]

Anyone who kills an highway man or a pirate is not punishable by whether he does it by his own hand, by issuing an order or by casting a vote. [B 260]

One should avenge to the best of one's ability those who are unjustly treated and not pass them by; for to do so is just and good not to do so unjust and bad. [B261].

The Socratic dialogues argue with these kinds of very dangerous recommendations by challenging the sophist under what criteria is used to determine what is virtue, who is a fool, who is a pirate, is a just man one who kills his enemies, who are his enemies, can stones think? The modern argument would be to excuse Democritus by considering he based his ideas of thought thousands of years ago, but Socrates argued equally thousands of years ago without this excuse that the views of the sophists are loose and opinionated conjecture .

If you hold with the theories of Democritus then you believe the stones are not only superior to your intellect they created it. The discovery of Plato's works gave a new authority to challenge the old antiquated authorities.

Symbolism

Symbolism is used with great effect in Tudor art there is a very informative web site written by Jack Leslau that has done some fabulous research on this which brings the Nostell portrait to life. Jack researched the courtly language of French homophones to unravel the hidden meanings within the portrait. His conclusions culminated with an intuitive decision that the "secretary or messenger carrying the scroll" was Dr John Clement alias Richard the Duke of York one of the princes allegedly killed in the Tower of London. He suggests that "heresius" [the name written above the messenger] in the homophone language is "heir" and subsequently "rightful heir". He considers the messenger is the highest placed person and thus the highest ranked he also carries a sword and buckler [small defensive sword and shield] which he interprets as "rai jante" regant. With a closer examination Henry Patenson or Elizabeth Dauncey could be fractionally higher; its hard to be sure the artist has made no clear distinction and the the vases of irises seam to want to take top rank. The sword and the buckler could easily be a symbol of Christian faith and a reference to *Enchiridion*, Erasmus's *"Education of a Christian Knight"*, but why the gesticulating middle finger which in vernacular language implies something rude? Then again is the messenger just carrying an heretical scroll?

Then again perhaps Jack's intuition is right and the portrait refers to a King the rightful hier but a very special kind of philosophical King bringing the new learning.

Jack uses several other symbols to reach his conclusions for example: - The covered vase is taken to be a reference by the artist to the expression "vase d'élection" or "The Chosen One" and the covering of the vase with a cloth suggests the artist did not like Margaret Clement, he paints her unflatteringly, and his opinion was "Le vase est couvert", meaning "The Chosen One is justified". Which again fits with the special kind of king.

The purple peony which is the medicinal plant he considers to be referring to the Dr being royal meaning Dr J Clement is royalty but the peony could just as easily be referring to the Medici Pope.

Jacks work is subjective, but there are still valuable ideas and the conspiracy theory brings added interest to the portrait which is to be encouraged.

By way of conjecture the inscription above John More in Latin "filius" [son] is misspelt to read "filuis" which if it is not a spelling mistake reads in the vernacular Thomas More is a type of scoundrel.

On the other hand it is well accepted that the traditional symbolism in the art world of a dog is a sign of the owners fidelity usually chosen to favour the sitter. The Nostell dogs were identified in 1731 by Rev J Lewis [Life and Death of Thomas More]. People have suggested they lack the quality of the whole composition but they have been no more poorly executed than the monkey and they do contribute to our understanding personally I sense they were added for good reasons.

The poor brown and white dog which sits slightly remote from the feet of Judge More the fur is very realistic. At one stage he was painted over thankfully he is now back as intended by the artist, he's quite relavent to the theme because he is cur dog. There is also a tradition that he is a spit turning dog which is also relavant.

The other dog which people suggest is almost human looking is a Bologna shock, which is a small breed of obedient Italian lap dog which Jack says has an eaves dropping cocked ear. It once had a crudely painted pig snout which as been cleaned off.

Then there countless other symbols like the glove, the open clock door, the weight suspended above Thomas More, the four ladies are pregnant and a tester bed in the back ground?

Jacks notices something interesting about the portico it's fleur de lis and cherubs which he refers to as Christian symbols of the hierachy of angels cherubim, seraphim and thrones - divine beings who symbolise justice.

Additionally within the same framework there are also two carved raised linen fold panels which might have an unclear referance to the ten commandments.

Jack does well to spot this hierachy of angels and they do symbolise divine beings and the justice of providence but they are not Christian they are pagan. Thomas More, Erasmus, Holbein and Cromwell would have known this because they are one of the reasons which ignited the Reformation.

The heirachy is the invention of a sixth century mystic who passed himself off has Dionysius the Areopagite mentioned in Acts 17;34. He also claimed that he was a witness to the crucifixion, a close friend of St John and other Saints. He got away with his deception for nearly nine hundred years his corpus of works were well read and respected by all the high authorities including John Colet, St John of the Cross, St Bonaventura, Master Eckart, Nicholas of Cusa, Albert the Great and St Thomas Aquinas who relied heavily on them in his *Summa theologiae*.

Uncovering these misnomers in Christian theology was one of the causes which contributed to the Reformation the main detective was Lorenzo Valla [1407–57] who realised that Dionysus the Areopagite was in fact a Neo Platonist, a very skilled one though. Dionysius blended hundreds of verses in almost equal numbers from the Old and New Testaments he then intersperses them with concepts and phrases from the works of Plato and the Neo Platonists presenting the whole as a completed linguistic jigsaw puzzle demonstrating how Judaeo - Christianity interrelates to Platonism. Following Valla's discovery of his hoaxes he became a fraudulent imposter.

Dionysius the Areopagite coined the term "hierarchy" in his Celestial Hierarchies which describes the celestial beings of angels who govern divine providence. The Celestial Hierarchies treaties suggests there is a difference between divine law and sacred scripture, he states "they are not mirrored".

"By such divine visions our venerable forefathers were instructed through meditation of celestial powers. Is it not told in holy scripture that the sacred law was given to Moses by God himself in order to teach us that in it is mirrored the divine and holy law"

This quote was taken from the Celestial Hierarchies Chapter IV [180D-181A] were the Areopagite describes the differences between the Greek numos [scriptural law] and thesmos divine laws handed down by angels.

The works of Dionysius the Areopagite suggest Christianity did not appear from nothing but took its roots and vocabulary from the earlier Hellenistic philosophies. His combined works illustrate how they interrelate, which means they are probably the earliest informed accurate and impartial reading of scripture that is available. On the other hand, his cunning ploy is so conspicuous it should have been rumbled much earlier. To explain Areopagite is the title of the chief judge of Athens residing at Mars Hill, quoted in Acts 17 were St Paul gives a rousing speech condemning the Hellenistic teaching of "the unknowable god". Consequently, the Areopagite becomes immediately converted to Christianity, yet the full corpus of Pseudo Areopagite fully supports the Platonist theology of the unknowable god making the works highly contradictory to the Pauline scriptures.

Nicholas of Cusa [1401–1464] was a great exponent of his teaching including the principle of *docta ignorantia* [the education of ignorance] the ineffability of god meaning true knowledge of god is a complete lack of knowledge, we can only describe god in terms of what he is not [*Via Negativa*]. The theory comes from Plato's Parmenides putting it simply if someone tells you they know god exists it can only be their opinion therefore in truth it is not feasible that god can exist, or if he does then he would be mere opinion, and could anyone in truth consider god to be just a matter of opinion? Incidentally Cusa also proposed heliocentrism long before Copernicus and Galileo.

The design for first Gothic Cathedrals originally called French style were inspired by the Pseudo Areopagite. Abbot Suger of St Denis (c. 1081 –

1151) was so transfixed by the numerous descriptions of celestial light contained within the treatise he felt compelled to build the Basilica, he even had carved into the nave a quote from the Celestial Hierarchies treatise "*For bright is that which is brightly coupled with the bright/and bright is the noble edifice which is pervaded by the new light*."

Additionally, his Divine Names treaties [DN 704D-705D] describing cosmic spirals and circles was the inspirational motive behind the heavenly domes of ecclesiastical buildings.

[Architectural Principles in the Age of Humanism. Page 10].

He even inspired the famous poem called "The cloud of Unknowing"

This all goes to demonstrate that the study of Plato is inspirational, the study of his pupil Aristotle is hopelessly drab.

The works of Plato and Aristotle were reaching Florence throughout the fifteenth century along with Neo Platonists commentaries including better quality copies of the Greek New Testaments. Lorenzo Valla's detective work did not just uncover the deception of Dionysius, Valla had a field day.

One of the major Papal frauds Valla discovered was the Donation Constantini: when the Emperor Constantine moved from Rome to his strategically safe capital of Constantinople, he agreed to give Pope Sylvester I the supremacy over the *sees* of Antioch, Alexandria, Constantinople, and Jerusalem and all the world's churches. This document granted administrative rights to Sylvester and the successive Popes over all estates and churches throughout the empire including the abandoned imperial palace in Rome. Most importantly, Constantine gave the Pope control of and all the regions of the Western Empire; ["west" includes the undiscovered Americas] this effectively implies that the Pope held the right to appoint Kings and Queens in the West. Hence the control of Henrys divorce.

Valla proved that the document could not possibly have been written in the historical era of Constantine the vernacular style dated conclusively to a later era [8th Century]. One of Valla's reasons was that the document contained the word "satrap" which he believed Romans such as Constantine I would not have used.

His last work was *Novum Testamentum ex diversorum utriusque linguae codicum collatione adnotationes* [Annotations on the New Testament] which sat gathering dust until Erasmus searched them out and published them; later publishing his own *Novum instrumentum* in 1515.

 The spur behind the Renaissance was because Lorenzo de' Medici [1449–92] offered a safe refuge to Platonist philosophers fleeing the Syrian diaspora. He formed a new Italian Platonic Academy In Florence headed by Marsilo Ficino [1433 – 1499] and Giovanni Pico della Mirandola [1463 –1494]. The academy translated and published the whole of Plato's works. For the first time in Latin Europe Plato's works were available and for the first time the authority of Aristotle could be challenged. All the Socratic dialogues rationally reason through discounting and rejecting the opinions of rhetoricians and sophist thinkers who held opinions equal to the three bandits. In a nutshell the powerful people with control, lands and the wealth i.e. the Hapsburgs who had for centuries been schooled with Aristotelian Scholastic beliefs, they were now being challenged by the vastly superior authority of Plato which makes them into a mockery exposing their weakness which causes a rapid new clambering for power and control.

Luther was a qualified scholastic preacher, with his stubbornness he would not accept any pagan influence into his doctoring, ironically even though he was rejecting paganism he was schooled to present argument with Aristotelian/Isocratic rhetoric.

The Scholastic brainwashing methods had evolved through the late 12th and the early 13th century with a growing interest in Aristotelianism with his works arriving via Moorish Spain. Dominican friar Albertus Magnus was enthusiastic and encouraged Thomas Aquinas to develop a Christian admixture theology. The theology he created was a salad bowl of Isocratic lettuce, Old and New Testament relish, tossed together with works of the Platonist Dionysius the Areopagite then garnished with the Aristotelian condiments.

The harmony he established between Aristotelianism and Christianity was not forced but achieved by a new understanding of philosophical principles. Basically, he used a BMW chassis, bolted on a Rolls Royce engine, covered it with Fiat body prayed for the best, when it didn't spark, he lost the keys and consequently everyone is bemused into thinking the hot rod is a wonderful ornament, but do we push or pull it, scratch our heads, tickle it under the bonnet, drink tea or appreciate the wonders of the human mind to confuse ourselves instead of keeping it simple.

All the religious false ideologies of theology can be summed up by Erasmus in this extract from *In Praise of Folly*.

Judge Folly speaks: *for who can conceive these things, unless he has spent at least six and thirty years in the philosophical and super-celestial whims of Aristotle and the Schoolmen? Add to these our logicians and sophists, a generation of men more prattling than an echo and the worst of them able to out chat a hundred of the best picked gossips. I conceive, how much satisfaction this Self-love, who has a sister also not unlike herself called Flattery.*

Extracts from Erasmus, Desiderius. The Praise of Folly Kindle Edition. Translated by John Wilson   1668

Reading Seneca's works it is clear there where pagan schools of philosophy spread throughout the Mediterranean free to teach in a relaxed open manner. With the ever increasing force of Judeo Christianity the pagans were persecuted, their heathen temples gradually destroyed and looted by zealot monks until the final Platonist school in Athens was closed in 529 AD. Luckily Plato's work was preserved by isolated groups in Arabia these groups in time came under further persecution. The Florentine academy fortunately just in time opened its doors to the remaining Byzantium humanists; even then there is a tale of a boat load of precious manuscripts sinking to the bottom of the sea. Such was the disastrous history of European culture, belligerently destroyed by Europeans who belligerently attempted the same the world over under the heraldic symbol of Christianity.

Utopia and the Aristotle influence

Utopia was first published and edited by Erasmus in 1516; at its onset Thomas More was heavily criticised and mocked for his poor Latin and grammar by a young French idealist poet called Germain de Brie. Brie was more popularly known as Brixius he had been a pupil of Janus Lascaris one of the original Greek refugees from Byzantine Constantinople who Lorenzo de' Medici welcomed to the Florentine academy. Lascaris had brought over 200 books of antiquities back to Florence and tutored Brixius in humanism. With his schooling Brie was an excellent linguist skilled in Latin and Greek but he was also a close friend of Erasmus. In outrage at the criticism More with his usual doctrinaire flair for a street brawl eagerly rushed into publishing an abusive counterattack, thinking Erasmus would rally to the cause because he after all he assisted with the publishing. Erasmus calmly washed his hands leaving More embarrassingly isolated in desperation he rushed to the printers to retrieve any unsold copies of his diatribe.

[From, John Guy *A Daughters Love page* 116]

When Erasmus assisted Thomas More with the publishing of Utopia there is no doubt, he knew what it represented and let him set himself up has a fool. Referring again to the Ulrich Von Hutten letter on Thomas More Erasmus reports: -

"*His Utopia was published with the aim of showing the causes of the bad condition of states; but was chiefly a portrait of the British State, which he has thoroughly studied and explored*".

The *thoroughly studied and explored* comment hints at the three bandits involvement in the English law education.

More's proposed Utopia is still considered by many modern scholars to be a model of an idealistic Christian state without evil, educated people making these silly comments need to consider that the Utopian slaves and women are insignificant, valueless, and subhuman. Does this not confirm Erasmus's point that, *none is less remote from the common feelings of humanity than the evil of Thomas More?* Is Thomas More the inspirational herald guiding men's souls to the virtue by way of his idealistic happy Christian Paradiso on Earth? Callously dehumanising his fellow human beings he truly became the English de-facto arbiter for immoral judgement.

Thomas Mores Utopia was given great accolades by the Soviet Union and was a huge influence on the advocates of communism.

Hailed as a Communist hero by Karl Marx, Friedrich Engels, and Karl Kautsky, Thomas More's contribution to "the liberation of humankind" is commemorated, at Lenin's suggestion, on a monument erected in 1918 in Aleksandrovsky Garden near the Kremlin.

Margaret L. King (2014). *Renaissance Humanism*: An Anthology of Sources.

Erasmus wrote to a friend in 1517 that he should send for More's *"Utopia, if he had not read it, and wished to see the true source of all political evils."*

And to Thomas More Erasmus wrote of his book, *"A burgomaster of Antwerp is so pleased with it that he knows it all by heart."*

More, Thomas. UTOPIA (Wisehouse Classics Edition) (p. 7). Wisehouse. Kindle Edition.

Utopia is often cited as a great Socratic dialogue inspired by Plato's Republic, the objective with this chapter is to demonstrate that Thomas More is primarily Aristotelian and whilst inspired by the Republic Utopia is fundamentally influenced by Aristotle's Politics. The recognisable difference is that Utopia is an evil state in perpetual readiness for war, all be it the Utopian's only fight just wars. In contrast Socrates argues that it can never be right to cause harm because of the injustice it causes to your soul he also rejects the belief *"that the stronger has the right to rule the weaker"* which is the underlying principle behind all slavery.

There is a strong possibility that Thomas More may have developed his idea for presenting the Utopian proposals in reaction to the Byzantium humanist Georgios Gimistos Plethon who wrote a now destroyed work called "Nomoi" a manifesto redefining social and political reform through revolutionary Platonic ideals of nonviolence. His popularist views called for a new world order and Thomas More's Utopia is possibly a one-upmanship response by going one better than the man who introduced Platonism to Europe. There is a section in Plato's Republic referred to as *the community of wives and children* which we are told by Erasmus was greatly admired by Thomas More and this is an obvious influence on Utopia. Thomas More as possibly leaped into his proposals thinking he can now show Plethon a thing or two about Plato. The Utopian state is comparable to the incongruous city state Plato's describes in the Republic. Academics therefore set Thomas More on a philosophical pedestal fabricating a myth that Utopia is comparable with the great Socratic discourses.

The problem lies with the myth surrounding *the community of wives and children* dialogue which can be found in book five of the Republic this is the cause of so much false understanding of the Republic, it is doubtful if academics will ever stop misquoting Plato. For example I listen quite often to the BBC radio series called *In or time* by Melvin Bragg with discussions by leading academics on popular subjects, one programme is dedicated to understanding the Republic from the comments made by the university professors it is clear they don't understand this dialogue.

Because of Erasmus's comments I started looking at the community and wives dialogue, I was completely lost, Socrates the pacifist suddenly begins advocating totalitarianism etc. There was no one I could find who could give me a lead to what it all meant. Plato in book five appears to be promoting state-controlled education, eugenics, infantilism, selective breeding, state militarisation, an elite guardian class, replacing the traditional family structure with institutional communities an end to the heterogeneous family life thus he has been called a racist presenting thee model for state tyranny. Reading Plato in a literal sense is fool hardy which unfortunately Thomas More despite all his legalistic training as also done just this and likewise countless others. It is a notorious dialogue which is the cause of so much confusion and mythology regarding Plato and the beautiful state of Callipolis. Ironically scholars, academics and politicians have hijacked Plato's works turning them into a rudimentary or a primitive principle for state government even belittling the proposals rather than understanding them as a dharma of Self-government. At the end of the next chapter we can discuss this further, but for now can you please except for the presentation of this chapter scholars are miss reading this strangely odd dialogue. Therefore some of the quotes I'm using for this chapter the authors are under the same impression that Thomas More's Utopia is on a par with Plato's beautiful state, which causes a great deal of confusion, if you could please bear this in mind and I will try to show you in the next chapter that in order to make an omelette Plato must crack eggs.

A close reading of the Republic will reveal the whole work is a dharma, gradually Socrates teaches you how to recognise a tyrant, but more importantly how to recognise the tyrant within. We all have these traits at times we all want to rule the world and believe we can soar with the gods. Even more importantly the Republic not only helps you recognise the tyrant within but how to kill the little beast which is what the psychologist called the overwhelming influx of god head meaning a hugely inflated ego.

Thomas More finds the Republic agreeable simply because he is miss reading the whole book and was only selectively reading the parts, he found understandable. There is an example of this when he translated the biographical life of Pico, he ignored the esoteric stuff *. Thomas More like many readers was not aware that Plato and Socrates are playing the devil's advocate, they are really mocking the totalitarian state with a deliberate set up to demonstrate how a sick state develops.

[* See page 76 of G Wegemer *Young Thomas More and the art of Liberty*]

That aside it is not the purpose here to deconstruct the proposals of Utopia, although it would be fun to do so. Mores model for Utopia is the recipe for an "A" typical tyrannical state which Erasmus quotes *"the true source of political evils"*.

Here's a quote from Utopia, *"punishment is thought necessary for striking terror into others. For the most part slavery is the punishment, even of the greatest crimes, for as that is no less terrible to the criminals themselves than death"*, unquote. Note the vague words of conjecture coming from the top lawyer in the country *"even of the greatest crimes"* in other words this does not exclude but includes any crime the punishment will be nevertheless slavery.

The next question would be how does he define crime for which the answer would be "anything" judge More or the ruler of Utopia decide.

A favourite tactic of tyrants is to make muddled statements which appeal to literal minds, but Thomas More is not the best at this deception, quote *"They do not make slaves of prisoners of war except those that are taken in battle"* unquote. Clearly this statement is a form of lie a flatulent deception which can be traced back to Thomas Mores scholastic education and legal profession.

Searching around the internet I found an article which will help it was written in 1976 in which the author was highly delighted he had discovered Utopia was fundamentally Aristotelian, believing the relationships between Aristotle and Thomas More to have been *slighted* by favouring Plato's influence. In his realisation that Utopia is Aristotelian the author of the article is modestly elated with himself and writes over forty pages of heavily referenced evidence to demonstrate their mutual passion for Aristotle. The only disadvantage to his comments is that he is reserving himself on account of going against the accepted scholarly view. Cautiously he says Utopia is influenced by several schools of philosophy in the tradition of Plato and Aristotle Politics, his study of Utopia aims to show in what way the writings of Aristotle Politics and Nicomachean Ethics may have had an impact on Utopia.

I have already laboured there is a mistaken myth surrounding Plato's *community of wives and children dialogue*, which Thomas I White the author of the article is not aware of and keeps considering Plato with Aristotle for this reason, but other than that he offers clear evidence Utopia is fundamentally an Aristotelian Politic inspired state.

The article begins: - *The obvious influence of Plato on Utopia and the antagonism of some humanists towards the medieval scholastics and their belief in the primacy of Aristotle seem to have resulted in the impression that Thomas More agrees with this anti-Aristotelianism and that Aristotle had little influence on Utopia. As a result, this matter has never been considered in depth and important points about Thomas More have been overlooked.*

Our elated scholar continues: -

More would have been introduced to Aristotle while at Oxford, and after returning to London, he probably received some impetus to continue studying the philosopher from his friends. Thomas Linacre, for example, had assisted with the Aldine Aristotle and lectured on the Meteorologica in London (about 1501), and a reference to these lectures in More's epistle to Martin Dorp suggests that More attended them. More's acquaintance with Aristotle is indicated by a number of explicit references to this thinker. Epigram 89 is entitled 'De Somno, e Graeco. Sententia Aristotelis' and its theme is repeated.

Further: Thomas More dedicated Utopia to his friend and colleague Bishop Cuthbert Tunstall 1474 – 18 November 1559 who was an English Scholastic.

Our author adds: -

Most telling, however, are passages in More's letter to Martin Dorp and Utopia. More professes in the epistle that Aristotle is a philosopher 'whom I love above many, but still along with many'. He rebukes Dorp only because he is overly devoted to the thinker ('you seem not only to cherish him above many, but also instead of many, indeed, instead of all', and he exhorts him to learn Greek, saying, '[Aristo tle] could never be completely known to you without a knowledge of Greek'. More asserts that 'there is no translation of Aristotle so suit able as to have the same powerful effect on one's spirit as does the original.

Thomas More's confident rebuke of Dorp is probably influenced because he has suddenly become a proud Platonist after wrongly reading the *community of wives and children dialogue* and joyfully waving the flag on Erasmus's humanist band wagon. Continuing the article, Thomas I White notes Utopia is a happy state everyone is happy and seeks a pleasurable life just as Aristotle's opinion: *a happy life is a virtuous life; a virtuous life is a pleasant life.*

For there to be profit in the world someone must lose, for every medicine there are always side effects and the happy life is no exception. For everyone to live the Utopian virtuously pleasurably happy life; slaves, not the citizens, do the menial tasks such as the of butchering animals because Thomas More considers that such constant slaughter dissipates the highest human Aristotelian virtue of *"mercy"*. Thomas More also criticises the practice of hunting as this cruelty leads to a certain habit of disposition in an individual. The Utopian slaves who are chained and kept in perpetual labour are obviously not human beings, their defined has citizens that are being punished for serious wrongdoing or those who have been condemned to death in other states, others are prisoners of war and some paupers from other countries who choose Utopia rather to live has slaves elsewhere. The state penal system of Utopia legislates; rather than execute criminals they must be enslaved for useful services for the enjoyment of the happy state.

However, the philanthropical nature of Thomas More equally parallels Aristotle's idealism that slaves should be treated well and always should have at least a hope of emancipation. Presumably after eating copious amounts of the emancipation carrots slaves miraculously transform into becoming virtuous humans. It would be correct opinion to assume that the benevolent justice system for Utopian slaves and criminals is idealistic "conjecture", just how this works in practice appears to be ambiguous guesswork.

Thomas I White's article draws alignment with Aristotle's opinions with suggestions that Thomas More charitably employs the notion of fairness, evenness, or equal treatment ('aequum') when he makes judgments about certain social practices and when he employs the concept of justice by conjecture.

"As both Aristotle and Thomas More are against the evil of tyranny, they consider an acceptable form of one-man rule is best, they both agree the unacceptable type of rule is tyranny. Thomas More and Aristotle agree that it is a policy of tyrants to keep their subjects poor so that they will have neither the means to support an army nor the leisure to plot against their ruler and second, that tyrants keep close watch upon all things that can produce pride and confidence in the people".

To their commendable merit both Aristotle and More are aware of the implications of tyrannical oppression; but unfortunately, they are unable to recognise these traits in their own opinions. The difference between a slave owner and a tyrant is something the author of the article, Thomas I White, Thomas More and Aristotle fail to define and their erudite belief in conjecture is that muddled thinking develops superbly superior muddled thinking.

For example, Aristotle's overall position on communism is that while property should be owned privately, it should be used as though it were held in common. Thomas I White further states: -

Utopian communism is very close to Plato's thinking, and Plato is severely criticized by Aristotle. It is interesting to note, however, that the disagreement between More and Aristotle does not seem to be based on a difference of opinion about human nature.

For our simple exercise Thomas I White provided more than enough evidence that More is an Aristotelian thinker. Unfortunately, repeatedly learned scholars miss read *the community of wives and children dialogue* this misconception is unstoppable until universities make a concerted effort to read Plato's Republic correctly and stop comparing his actual Callipolis with the draconian proposals of book five.

The article concludes:- *Nevertheless , since there is some ideas in Utopia which almost certainly come from Aristotle and since there are important similarities and dissimilarities between the two thinkers is such a wide range of ideas it is reasonable to conclude that More was significantly influenced by Aristotle That is to say as one of Mores sources Aristotle not only provides an occasional argument or detail but also was a major force in the development of certain ideas to Utopia.*

Aristotle and Utopia Author(s): Thomas I. White Source: Renaissance Quarterly, Vol. 29, No. 4 (Winter, 1976), pp. 635-675 Published by: The University of Chicago Press on behalf of the Renaissance Society of America.

Lastly Thomas I White says *"It is important to note that despite all that has been said about the importance of the Republic to Utopia, More's remarks about justice do not seem to have any relation to Plato's theory of justice. Nowhere in Utopia does More speak about justice either in terms of Plato's notion of justice in the state (doing one's own proper work), or justice in the individual (internal order of the soul). Since this is the central concept of the Republic, it is no small matter for More to reject Plato's discussion of justice for Aristotle's. This extremely telling point supports my earlier contention that Thomas More is fundamentally an eclectic thinker".*

Leaving the comments of Thomas I White behind a notable attraction for the state of Utopia is it defence strategy; strategically it is an impenetrable island geographically placed to naturally form a defensive against its attackers.

Thomas More says the Utopians detest war as a very brutal thing they only fight just wars which they define through…. Can you guess? ….. yes you got it,….. divine conjecture.

Yet they do not rashly engage in war, unless it be either to defend themselves or their friends from any unjust aggressors, or, out of good nature or in compassion to assist an oppressed nation in shaking off the yoke of tyranny. They, indeed, help their friends not only in defensive but also in offensive wars; but they never do that unless they had been consulted before the breach was made, and, being satisfied with the grounds on which they went, they had found that all demands of reparation were rejected, so that a war was unavoidable

I have already stated the Republic teaches how to recognise tyranny therefore we should make a particular note of how the Utopians honour their nobility: just like the *community of wives and children* they erect statues to the memories of such worthy men who have deserved well of their country, and set these in their market-places, both to perpetuate the remembrance of their actions and to be an incitement to their posterity to follow their example.

Utopia only defines justice on the level of fairness in the conjectured sense. Any consideration that justice is other than a legal term completely goes straight over Thomas Mores head. Justice in the Republic is defined as when the three parts of the soul mind their own business [Rep 441d] What Socrates really means is the house that wisdom builds is self-mastery [Rep 443e] which when we fully grasp he infers a dharma a nonviolent way of life a kin to philosophical hatha yoga taught by the Sanatan schools.

An examination of Utopia will soon discover there are three classes of people, the Prince who is elected for life he makes the laws, the privileged ruling class administer the laws, the peasant working class who obey the laws and then there are the subhuman donkey class slaves who dream of a paradise paved with carrots.

The fettered slaves do all filthy sordid work for carrots and do not receive any education. The elders educate the peasants with frequent lectures in morality meaning they undertake brainwashing indoctrinations, indeed there would be no liberal arts studies as this would be too taxing for their little brains. Remember this is a happy Christian state were everything is state owned even the women, women are married off like cattle, marriage is all arranged by the state, if a family has to many children they will be forcibly removed, if the population becomes large in one area they will be forcibly transferred to another, all work is strictly enforced by law , idleness is not permitted, punishment for adultery is slavery, the punishment for crime is slavery, because putting people to death is wasteful because their labour is more useful, people quickly learn the rules so this make governance of the state easier, thus there are less laws and everyone is obedient to the elders, thus judge More will only need to work the odd shift. Spare time is to be used for improvement of minds classed as moral improvement, there are no luxuries, no taverns, no gambling, everyone wears the same plain wool clothes, the slaves are decorated and festooned with worthless gold, every city is the same, every house is the same, if you wish to travel you need permission from the prince, if caught without permission punishment is slavery and the list of barbarities goes on and on. But I thought it best give you some other tasters of the happy Christian state in the words of Saint Thomas: -

1) Who, if they are but to buy a horse of a small value, are so cautious that they will see every part of him, and take off both his saddle and all his other tackle, that there may be no secret ulcer hid under any of them, and that yet in the choice of a wife, on which depends the happiness or unhappiness of the rest of his life, a man should venture upon trust, and only see about a hands breadth of the face, all the rest of the body being covered, under which may lie hid what may be contagious as well as loathsome. All men are not so wise as to choose a woman only for her good qualities, and even wise men consider the body as that which adds not a little to the mind, and it is certain there may be some such deformity covered with clothes as may totally alienate a man from his wife, when it is too late to part with her; if such a thing is discovered after marriage a man has no remedy but patience; they, therefore, think it is reasonable that there should be good provision made against such mischievous frauds.

2) "Their women are not married before eighteen nor their men before two-and-twenty, and if any of them run into forbidden embraces before marriage they are severely punished, and the privilege of marriage denied them unless they can obtain a special warrant from the Prince.

3) Husbands have power to correct their wives and parents to chastise their children, unless the fault is so great that a public punishment is thought necessary for striking terror into others. For the most part slavery is the punishment even of the greatest crimes, for as that is no less terrible to the criminals themselves than death, so they think the preserving them in a state of servitude is more for the interest of the commonwealth than killing them, since, as their labour is a greater benefit to the public than their death could be, so the sight of their misery is a more lasting terror to other men than that which would be given by their death. If their slaves rebel and will not bear their yoke and submit to the labour that is enjoined them, they are treated as wild beasts that cannot be kept in order, neither by a prison nor by their chains, and are at last put to death. But those who bear their punishment patiently, and are so much wrought on by that pressure that lies so hard on them, that it appears they are really more

4) "They do not make slaves of prisoners of war, except those that are taken in battle, nor of the sons of their slaves, nor of those of other nations: the slaves among them are only such as are condemned to that state of life for the commission of some crime, or, which is more common, such as their merchants find condemned to die in those parts to which they trade, whom they sometimes redeem at low rates, and in other places have them for nothing. They are kept at perpetual labour, and are always chained, but with this difference, that their own natives are treated much worse than others: they are considered as more profligate than the rest, and since they could not be restrained by the advantages of so excellent an education, are judged worthy of harder usage. Another

sort of slaves are the poor of the neighbouring countries, who offer of their own accord to come and serve them: they treat these better, and use them in all other respects as well as their own countrymen, except their imposing more labour upon them, which is no hard task to those that have been accustomed to it; and if any of these have a mind to go back to their own country, which, indeed, falls out but seldom, as they do not force them to stay, so they do not send them away empty-handed.

5) *The education of youth belongs to the priests, yet they do not take so much care of instructing them in letters, as in forming their minds and manners aright; they use all possible methods to infuse, very early, into the tender and flexible minds of children, such opinions as are both good in themselves and will be useful to their country, for when deep impressions of these things are made at that age,*

6) *"None of the magistrates have greater honour paid them than is paid the priests; and if they should happen to commit any crime, they would not be questioned for it; their punishment is left to God, and to their own consciences; for they do not think it lawful to lay hands on any man, how wicked so ever he is, that has been in a peculiar manner dedicated to God; nor do they find any great inconvenience in this, both because they have so few priests, and because these are chosen with much caution, so that it must be a very unusual thing to find one who, merely out of regard to his virtue, and for his being esteemed a singularly good man, was raised up to so great a dignity, degenerate into corruption and vice; and if such a thing should fall out, for man is a changeable creature, yet, there being few priests, and these having no authority but what rises out of the respect that is paid them, nothing of great consequence to the public can proceed from the indemnity that the priests enjoy.*

Aristotle is Thomas Mores favoured philosopher and Utopia is fundamentally Aristotelian, there is not one single Socratic paraphrase of wisdom or the love of Sophia or even a hint that Thomas More vaguely understands the meaning of wisdom in the entire work.

We can learn a great deal about ourselves from the study of Thomas More but we have to be honest, commentators who bull up his work with blinded statements that Utopia is a Socratic dialogue embodying all the humanist convictions of the age or one of the finest contribution to English prose, ranking it alongside the greats in English literature do not offer any insight and in fact do his work a disservice he would have wanted us to learn from his failures. His work was written to a poor standard Latin and as for Socratic dialogue it does not even warrant a response. We must learn and be prepared to face the truth Thomas More was an extraordinary gifted orator all his exponents proclaim this. Plato's dialogues are written to demonstrate and recognise that all orators dress up their tyranny with different disguises. We all have these psychological traits and behave like tyrants at times, extreme characters like Thomas More help us learn about inner ourselves but we must be honest, and with that we can even poke fun at ourselves.

Thomas More in 2000 was given the posthumous honour of "Saint of politicians" as we know for a politician to achieve power, they generally must become good public speakers which we call orators or rhetoricians, Socrates calls them sophists and the great Socratic dialogues are written against their tyrannically held beliefs.

Poor Thomas More has not grasped that an exponent of slavery is an exponent of tyranny, the practice of slavery is the most extreme form of tyranny and advocated by his mentor Aristotle.

The whip of shock and awe ideology in Aristotle Politics and Thomas Mores Utopian society makes everyone happy because using this remedy if your wife or your slave is not happy you beat the hell out of them preferably making an example of them in public then they soon get the idea and everyone else does. However, both men are keen to stress punishment should only be used in moderation, "*yes boss I understand* boss that's why I'm grateful you're a good boss who only gave me twenty-five lashings."

To quote Aristotle Nicomachean Ethics: The Father of the house rules his wife, children and slaves are not part of the state there is no appeal for injustice to the state for protection because they are a man's chattels, biological tools. This is just one quote from some 380 pages of drab dribble.

From the dialogue on Justice; *Justice of a master is not the same as although it is analogous to the forms already discussed. There cannot be injustice in an unqualified sense towards that which is one's own and chattel or a child until it is of a certain age and has attained independence, as it were a part of oneself; and nobody choses to injure himself hence there can be no injustice towards oneself and so neither can there be any conduct towards them that is politically just or unjust For political justice is as we saw defined by law and is found in communities where law is naturally accepted those whose members share equally in ruling and being ruled. Hence justice is more fully realised between husband and wife than between father and children or master and slave it is in fact domestic justice, but this too is distinct from political justice.*

We must not forget in Utopia the prince owns everything therefore he cannot possibly do injustice to his subjects. Aristotle Politics is a similar sized book, full of the same screwed up despotic thinking, that ruled medieval Europe here are a few quotes: -

A possession may be considered in the same nature as a part of anything now a part is not only a part of something but also is nothing else so is a possession therefore a master is only the master of the slave but no part of him but the slave is not only slave of the master but nothing else but that. This fully explains what is the nature of a slave and what capacities for that being who by nature is nothing of himself but totally another's and is a man is a slave by nature and that man who is the property of another is his mere chattel though he continues a man but a chattel is an instrument for use separate from body.

Since then some men are slaves by nature and others are freemen where slavery is advantageous to anyone then it is just to make him a slave.

..... government is that which a master exercises over a slave. But to govern ill is disadvantageous to both; government is that which is useful to the part and to the whole to the body and to the soul, but the slave is as it were a part of the master's if it were an animated part of his body though separate. For which mutual unity must exist between master and slave.

As a slave is a particular species of property let us inquire into the nature of property in general............ As nature therefore makes nothing imperfect or vain it is necessarily follows that she has made all these for men: for which reason what we gain in war is in a certain degree a naturally acquisition ; for hunting is a part of it which is necessary for us to employ against wild beasts and those men who being intended by nature for slavery are unwilling to submit to it war is by nature just......

To conclude Luther's received his doctorate from a Scholastic professorship with the usual endorsements from the scholastic Aristotelian textbook of Peter Lombard. With this Luther advocated the study of Aristotle, he lectured on the *ethics* of Aristotle. He developed his new Christian theology by adamantly rejecting the pagan philosophy of Plato along with Aristotle, but he still retained the scholastic imprint within his psychological make up. More and Luther locked horns like two rutting stags with belligerent attitudes to each other trampling their views across the plains of Europe.

Our next task is to define wisdom, philosophy and humanities, but first here are a couple more extracts from the Von Hutten letter.

"How happy the states would be if the ruler everywhere put magistrates like More in office! Meanwhile he has acquired no trace of haughtiness".

"Such is More even in the Court. And then there are those who think that Christians are to be found only in monasteries"!...

Erasmus, Desiderius. Delphi Collected Works of Desiderius Erasmus (Illustrated) (Delphi Series Nine Book 12) . Delphi Classics. Kindle Edition.

Humanites

Thomas More believed that to train the soul for virtue there must be a diligent and demanding study of liberal arts: -

Quote: *To prepare the soul for virtue without proper training, reason would run "riot, and wax over high-hearted and proud, [and would] not fail to fall in rebellion.*

Gerard Wegemer is one of the present-day authorities on the life and works of Thomas More, below he confirms our discovery that More was convicted to the opinions of Aristotle, stressing the importance of a liberal art education to train the soul for virtue.

Quote*: More recommends a good education in the liberal arts to "prepare the soul for virtue" (CW15 139). Without proper training, reason would run "riot, and wax over high-hearted and proud, [and would] not fail to fall in rebellion," even against its own firmest convictions. To mitigate the chance of this rebellion, More recommends diligent and demanding study of the liberal arts, with special attention to the great poets (CW15 139, SL 99) and "true philosophy, especially Aristotle" (SL 18), if one is to acquire the level of sound judgment that will not "swerve from the very nature of things" (SL 23). Such training will lead people to moderate their expectations and to see the difficulty of making political judgments. One must understand deeply these difficulties and the contingency of temporal affairs if one is to avoid rashness and pride. To "learn prudence in human affairs," More "doubt[s] that any study contributes as richly to this practical skill as the study of poets, orators, and histories" (CW15 139). More's strongest scorn and satire is for those who presumptuously overlook the difficulties in such judgment; he* *compares them to the proud rooster who "puffs up his chest while strutting in his own dung-pit" (SL 39). Such people are unable to see the law of nature imprinted in their own hearts, since vain fantasies fill their sight.*

This short extract was taken from the internet posting titled The Political Philosophy of Sir Thomas More Gerard Wegemer University of Dallas, which in turn was a extract from: -

Saints, Sovereigns, and Scholars: Studies in Honor of Frederick D. Wilhelmsen. Edited by R. A. Herrera, James Lehrberger, M. E. Bradford. New York: Peter Lang, 1993, pp. 137-143. Reprinted with permission, with minor corrections.

With every word Mores Aristotlian indoctrination stands out, the question is why would anyone not want a rebellious soul or try to overpower it or believe it needs to be trained? It is astonishing every word quoted above is a rejection of non violent Platonic philosophy. The convictions of Thomas More in this address are therefore counterintuitevly an advocation for the acceptance of violence, consider the words he uses: overpower, rebellious and training there all domineering controlling measures consistant with slavery. Which means there is major problem when reading Renaissance and Reformation history because historians and politicians are giving their opinions without fully grasping the fundamentals of humanist philosophy.

Needless to say confusion abounds, if we can start by trying to define the of study of humanities: Traditionally a humanist is defined by a person who studies the classic works of the Greeks and Romans to enrich his Christian beliefs this study further becomes defined as the liberal art studies of the trivium and quadrivium or simply the *Studia humanitatis.*

A typical definition would be: -

Liberal arts are *those subjects or skills that in classical antiquity were considered essential for a free person (liberalis, "worthy of a free person") to know in order to take an active part in civic life, something that (for ancient Greece) included participating in public debate, defending oneself in court, serving on juries, and most importantly, military service.*

Grammar, logic, and rhetoric were the core liberal arts (the trivium), while arithmetic, geometry, the theory of music, and astronomy also played a – somewhat lesser – part in education (as the quadrivium) this became the educational foundation for the schooling of European elites, the functionaries of political administration, the clergy of the various legally recognized churches, and the learned professions of law and medicine.

Cicero originally coined the term and introduced the *"studia humanitatis"* to Roman politics after studying how the Greeks taught the philosophy of Plato which challenge the religious dogma and ritual of his day. Here is how he describes his new science of humanity.

Cicero's De Republic: *"What command, what office, what kingdom can be preferred to that condition of mind, which looking down upon all things human, and esteeming them to be the objects of an inferior wisdom, turns ever to the contemplation of those things that are divine and eternal: persuaded that they only deserve to be called men, who are refined by the sciences of humanity? That which has been said of Plato, or of some other sage, appears to me therefore very excellent".*

Notice the godfather of *studia humanitatis* rejects liberal art studies in favour of the eternal Platonic wisdom and that wisdom is not man's wisdom because man's wisdom is inferior. Cicero does not even consider learning the trivium or the quadrivium important what is important to him is the *"condition of mind"* the true kingdom.

My reading of Cicero is that he is not a totally lily-white person when it comes to violence against fellow humans which complicates the matter, but he knows that Platonism is a study of "wisdom" meaning a contemplation of the eternal and not a study of traditional liberal arts. By introducing this study Cicero is also rejecting religious dogmas, but he further calls for an *educated citizenry* for the way for peace. [see quote below]

Out of interest the teachings of Eastern philosophy Ishvara is the eternal principle and Nashvara the decaying principle, on this point there appears to be a correlation between Cicero's interpretation of Plato and traditional Eastern wisdom. To quote Plato: -

The philosophical nature always love that learning which discloses to them something of the Being that always "Is" and does not wander about in generation or decay. [Rep 485b]

When Erasmus published *The Education of a Christian Prince* in 1516, he counselled the young prince to follow the wisdom philosophy of Plato, specifically rejecting the philosophy that argues about physical things in favour of the study of eternal powers.

Quote; *"not that philosophy, I mean that , which argues about elements and primal matter and motion and the infinite, but that which frees the mind from the false opinions of the multitude and from wrong desires and demonstrations the principles of right government by reference to the example set by the eternal powers".*

[Lisa Jardine transcription of *The Education of a Christian Prince*].

Erasmus agrees with Cicero the study of primal matter of the phenomenal world opposes the study of the eternal, therefore we can detect that Thomas More cannot be a humanist because Wegemer asserts More promoted the study of the physical liberal arts representing decay and generation. Noting both Cicero and Erasmus advocate Plato's *studia humanitatis* which is a learning of the eternal kingdom.

Confusion still abounds because by rejecting liberal art studies this goes against the scholarly view of humanism, to enable us to solve the puzzle for further clarification we can dig a little deeper, Erasmus petitions the Christian Prince to be nonviolent by gaining an understanding of Plato's philosophy which presupposes the alternative studies of primal matter involving physical things becomes the cause of anger and violence but also the studies must represent religious dogmas and rituals remembering the objective of Cicero was to replace these and of course this is the objective of Erasmus.

This may be still confusing because traditionally the study of liberal sciences was always promoted as the essential backbone of a good public-school education this principle is well established for giving a good rounded education. Erasmus specifically advises the Christian Prince not to study that philosophy of primal matter his book is a total rejection of the teachings of Isocratic rhetoric. This presupposes Isocrates must advocate the study of physical liberal sciences and is opposed to Plato's eternal study, but who is he?

Over the last two thousand Isocrates has been the greatest influence by far on Western education which in turn nourishes Western political, philosophical, religious, social and economic thinking. The biblical and encyclopaedic *The Oxford Companion to Philosophy*: does not even mention the leading authority who is the source of it all, but Erasmus is aware of his influence he wrote a full book against his dogmas. Socrates forms the Republican "city of speech" on the approval of Adeimantus [Rep 427d] who holds the Isocratic belief in rhetoric, which is why Thomas More approved the Republic city of speech.

The mentor of Aristotle was Isocrates he originally formed his school for teaching aspiring politicians and military leaders the art of rhetoric and oratory which later became Aristotle's gymnasium known as the Lyceum. We can also note that a *gymnastic education* must also encompass the traditional liberal art studies because this what the Lyceum gymnasium was used for, not just boxing and wrestling.

Isocrates is a true mercenary he is not interested in education for everyone he only considers that the elite rich and powerful the best people are entitled to an education the people who can afford to pay. Specifically, his pupils paid to be trained in rhetoric which included the original format of liberal arts. It goes without saying with an elite education system the elite will become ever more rich and powerful ever inventing new ways of exploiting the poor in an ever-competitive environment for survival of the fittest deviants all clambering for their greater share of the puddings. Which is the root of why his education system is the cause of wars, Plato, Cicero and Erasmus advocate eternal wisdom and universal education for peace, Isocrates dismisses this in favour of jungle mentality, but deceptively he always claims he advocates peace. *"We know you always want to restore the peace boss, because that is why you're a good boss so much better than those other bad bosses".*

Obviously, we have found a major difference between the common understanding of humanities and the original Ciceronian/Platonic understanding, this is not the only instance simple terms like philosophy and wisdom are riddled with confusion and misunderstanding, double meanings which Erasmus terms them. The cross-purpose language between the philosophy of Plato and opinion of Aristotle turns into a kind of game between their mentors Socrates v Isocrates, we will see examples of this later.

Historically there must be an interrelated pun on the two names Isocrates and Socrates because they represent totally opposing views, one generation and decay and the other eternal.

Whichever way we look Thomas More representing a good traditional liberal art education for the elite to prepare the soul for virtue and against rebellion seems to be missing the mark. He most certainly advocates violence and incites violence his training and beliefs are the traditional Aristotelian related views of wisdom formed by conjecture, which presupposes they are the wrong kind of study of virtue. In his ideal state Utopia, there is no petition for universal education, yet Cicero believes the way to peace is universal education for all.

Clearly we have stumbled upon a major difference which we need to clarify, to further investigate the relationship with nonviolence and the oppression imposed by liberal art studies we can take a look at the book of Gerard B Wegemer *"The Young Thomas More and the Arts of Liberty"* the opening paragraph begins: -

"In 1515 as part of their plan for international peace Thomas More and Erasmus both called for a renaissance - a rebirth – of the so-called liberal studies That so called referred to Seneca's famous statement: Hence you

see why liberal studies are so called: because they are the studies worthy of the free. But there is only one really liberal study, that which gives a person his liberty. It is the study of wisdom…. He adds: *In calling for this renaissance they were agreeing with their classical predecessors that education in the liberal arts or what Cicero often called studia humanitatis is the best path to lead to a state of peace because fostering of a virtuous and educated citizenry provides the key to peace and liberty".*

Here Wagemer is quoting from Seneca's Moral letters to Lucilius epistles 88.

This adds more confusion on one hand Wagemer says Thomas More and Erasmus both call for a rebirth of liberal studies, but on the other hand he says this study is "wisdom". Clearly Wegemer is confused and confuses his readers, he supports Thomas More and is trying to elevate his status by placing him shoulder to shoulder with the great man Erasmus and even standing him on the shoulders of the giants Seneca and Cicero, but is not aware that Plato, Erasmus, Cicero and now Seneca are advocating an entirely different study of wisdom one that rejects the liberal arts.

Erasmus was very knowledgeable regarding Seneca he had been employed transcribing his works to a higher standard of Latin for the Aldine press this plan for peace must have been instigated by Erasmus, Thomas More for prestige reasons is merely bumming a lift on the humanist band wagon.

To foster a virtuous population in the plan for peace Cicero includes an *educated citizenry* but Utopian education is elitist that espoused by three tyrant educators Isocrates Aristotle and Democritus. Which presupposes elitist education is not going to return international peace but just the opposite.

Confusion continues to abounds let's start again: *there is only one study that that is worth of the free that is "wisdom"* which is a study of the eternal confirmed by Erasmus, Cicero and Seneca, this means all the studies we normally associate with liberal arts are opposed to the art of liberty and do not contribute to peace. Oddly Wegemer the expert on Thomas More does not appear to separate out the two studies, either in the title of the book, the above quotes or within the entire book on the contrary he praises Thomas More, because he promoted *liberal art studies worth lofty noble and free*. The solution is to spot the term "rebellious soul", the liberal studies of Aristotle and co apply the chains of slavery and force the soul into becoming obedient to their understanding of virtue. A study of the eternal would remind the soul that it is a slave and prisoner for the benefit of the individual and cause the soul to become rebellious reminding it of its true home. The soul is pre-programmed with its divine nature we are the ones who cause it to become imprisoned by seeking self-aggrandisement.

Many people like Wegemer praise More for being an enlightened humanist because he believed in the education of his children particularly the girls. Cited below in authentic vague language of conjecture are Thomas More's valiant bragging rights on how he educated his children, but for the most part Erasmus was the biggest influence on the family education. It was he who carefully vetted William Gunnell their general house tutor and he probably planted the maggot into More's head that the girls must be educated in the new learning, More probably felt obligated has he was ever keen to be seen sailing on the popularist humanist flagship. Erasmus even enlisting the astronomer Nicholas Kratzer to be their tutor. Confirmation of all this came from Meg who quoted Erasmus was their educator and mentor in liberal arts.

Thomas More views on his children's education Quote; *"I could never endure to see you cry. You know for example how often I kissed you, how seldom I whipped you. My whip was invariably a peacocks tail. Even this I wielded hesitantly and gently so that sorry welts might not disfigure your tender seats. Brutal and unworthy to be called father is he who does not himself weep at the tears of his child".* Yours most sincerely Thomas More

[Quoted from *Family sex and marriage in England 1500-1800* Lawrence Stone page 119].

[For the education of More's children *A Daughters Love*; John Guy pages 59 and 67].

Erasmus was fully aware of the study of Plato's "wisdom" and knew the study of trivium and quadrivium is the cause of bondage not liberation because the reasoning is fundamental to Platonic philosophy. The evidence for this can be found particularly in *"In Praise of Folly"* in which we can see examples of his love of Platonic wisdom which is the case in all his works.

This study of Platonic wisdom is that which Erasmus terms *Bonae litterae* the new learning. Suddenly you begin to see common sense does not make any sense, the learning of "wisdom" rejects all the learning of education which we have been traditionally taught from childhood to believe is the right way to train the soul for virtue. Traditional teaching stems from Isocratic rhetoric which is where the public-school systems evolved from. Our education is geared to fostering his herd mentality we are not taught we are trained. To understand the art of wisdom means scrapping all you have been taught, it is important to realise learning liberal arts are the yoke of "bondage" and true wisdom is the only liberating study. Aristotle and slavery go together the master is chained to a fixed belief that he must control and train everything he is just as much a slave has the slave. Emancipation can only take place when mental attachment for controlling corporal things is removed and the soul can become rebellious and break free of the body prison. [Liberation]

If we examine the quoted Seneca letter in a little more detail you may grasp this further

"You have been wishing to know my views with regard to liberal studies [trivium and quadrivium] *My answer is this: I respect no study, and deem no study good, which results in money-making. Such studies are profit-bringing occupations, useful only in so far as they give the mind a*

preparation and do not engage it permanently. One should linger upon them only so long as the mind can occupy itself with nothing greater; they are our apprenticeship, not our real work. Hence you see why "liberal studies" are so called; it is because they are studies worthy of a free-born gentleman. But there is only one really liberal study, – that which gives a man his liberty. It is the study of wisdom, and that is lofty, brave, and great-souled. All other studies are puny and puerile. You surely do not believe that there is good in any of the subjects whose teachers are, as you see, men of the most ignoble and base stamp? We ought not to be learning such things; we should have done with learning them.

Seneca regards the study of wisdom is great souled all other studies are puerile taught by men of ignoble base stamp. Following this he asks the question *"But which of these paves the way to virtue,* and answers the question: *do such men teach virtue, or not? If they do not teach it, then neither do they transmit it. If they do teach it, they are philosophers"*

The evidence suggests that Thomas More must have been illiterate he has signed up for a plan for peace and does not have the foggiest clue. Wegemer quoting Seneca's letter is making point that Thomas More professes the value of liberal studies to gain the gift of "virtue", but according to Seneca with these studies he would be unable to transmit any virtue and is *most ignoble*.

Recapping so far, we have found that Plato/Socrates, Seneca, Cicero, Erasmus and Eastern philosophy all rejecting liberal arts for the study of virtue.

Going back to the letter by Seneca he proceeds to ridicule the teaching of geometry, mathematics, astronomy, wrestling, boxing and war preparations which all have no teaching with regards virtue.

This list presupposes because of the rejection that these are the gymnastic studies of Aristotle and Isocrates that they taught at the Lyceum.

Finally, Seneca continues the letter until comically he confuses himself with the philosophy of Parmenides and Zeno regarding the absolute "One" which does not exist. Undoubtably Seneca is referring to Platonic wisdom of the eternal that simply "is" which does not exist in our phenomenal world of generation, opinion and decay.

If both Seneca and Cicero are quoting Plato's eternal wisdom naturally for an understanding, we must go to the first-hand source. These definitions can be found in the Phaedo were Socrates throws our common sense completely out of the window. Therefore, first it is probably better to see how his rival Isocrates defines wisdom and philosophy.

To begin "Speech" is sacrosanct to Isocrates the holy of holies. All the great Socratic dialogues counterattack the rhetoricians because words and their meanings are deceptive conjecture and this exposure plays a major role in the Republic. The god who contrived speech is Hermes the god of tricksters, thieves and liars which give us an indication of where Isocratic ideology may take us. [Cratylus 408a]

Isocrates is the godfather of rhetoric and is literally prepared to defend "speech" come what may which presupposes his god is Hermes. This may appear to be immaterial and a pointless digression however it turns into revealing the key to unlock a very serious problem. The things to take note of with any Isocratic quotes are the *importance of speech, his vague ill-defined language, belief that the stronger rules the weaker* which epitomises the ideological cause of slavery, *pride of honours, truth of conjecture or opinion, speech as a guide, speech as a deception and the need for possession or control.* Most importantly "speech" in every case is also superior to intellect: -

"I maintain also that if you compare me with those who profess to turn men to a life of temperance and justice, you will find that my teaching is more true and more profitable than theirs. For they exhort their followers to a kind of virtue and wisdom which is ignored by the rest of the world and is disputed among themselves; I to a kind which is recognized by all.

They, again, are satisfied if through the prestige of their names they can draw a number of pupils into their society ; I, you will find, have never invited any person to follow me, but endeavour to persuade the whole state to pursue a policy from which the Athenians will become prosperous themselves, and at the same time deliver the rest of the Hellenes from their present ills" [Antidosis 85]

"And, if there is need to speak in brief summary of this power, we shall find that none of the things which are done with intelligence take place without the help of speech, but that in all our actions as well as in all our thoughts speech is our guide, and is most employed by those who have the most wisdom." [Antidosis 256]

"It follows, then, that the power to speak well and think right will reward the man who approaches the art of discourse with love of wisdom and love of honours. Furthermore, mark you, the man who wishes to persuade people will not be negligent as to the matter of character ; no, on the contrary, he will apply himself above all to establish a most honourable name among his fellow-citizens ; for who does not know that words carry greater conviction when spoken by men of good repute than when spoken by men who live under a cloud, and that the argument which is made by a man's life is of more weight than that which is furnished by words ? " Therefore, the stronger a man's desire to persuade his hearers, the more zealously will he strive to be honourable and to have the esteem of his fellow-citizens". [Antidosis 277-8]

"Now I have spoken and advised you enough on these studies for the present. It remains to tell you about "wisdom" and "philosophy."" It is true that if one were pleading a case on any other issue it would be out of place to discuss these words (for they are foreign to all litigation), but it is appropriate for me, since I am being tried on such an issue, and since I hold that what some people call philosophy is not entitled to that name, to define and explain to you what philosophy, properly conceived, really is. My view of this question is, as it happens, very simple. For since it is

not in the nature of man to attain a science by the possession of which we can know positively what we should do or what we should say, in the next resort I hold that man to be wise who is able by his powers of conjecture to arrive generally at the best course, and I hold that man to be a philosopher who occupies himself -with the studies from which he will most quickly gain that kind of insight." What the studies are which have this power I can tell you, although I hesitate to do so"... [The studies are the art of discourse being able to talk] [Antidosis 270]

[All the Antidosis quotes are from the Loeb]

We can reasonably confirm that Isocrates is a man who considers wisdom to be the study of conjecture and the meaning of philosophy is conjecture. Isocrates is a man confidently overflowing with belief in vague conjecture. He is the man who invented politics which he phrases above, *I have never invited anyone to follow me, but endeavour to persuade the whole state to pursue my policies.* Thankfully you can rest confidently with the assurance that whole of Western civilisation followed his Isocratic ideology of "speech" and subsequently the whole world has adopted his dogma of conjecture.

Digressing the banter can be quite funny at times, Isocrates refers to his opponents Plato and Socrates has "empty minded", "men who live under a cloud", "men who let their wits go wool gathering". The Socratic dialogues are discourses in which the pros and cons are discussed and refuted typically the Parmenides therefore Isocrates made this statement *"For they exhort their followers to a kind of virtue and wisdom which is ignored by the rest of the world and is disputed among themselves".*

Now we are ready to compare the Isocratic definitions with the invisible studies of the woolly-headed empty heads who study nothing.

To begin education in Socratic philosophy is a "paideia" similar to the meaning of the Eastern term Upanishad to sit together and discuss therefore Socratic discourses, involve group discussions which are more thought provoking and vastly superior to Isocratic lectures which are long winded speeches between himself and his own opinions.

By way of introduction Socrates in the Phaedo defines the definitions which you will discover philosophy is the art of dying and wisdom is the study of separating the soul from the body without the aid of the senses which means philosophy is a kin to Eastern philosophy of Samadhi letting go of the attachment to earthly possessions. Here are just a couple of quotes from the Phaedo which clarify the Socratic definitions of wisdom and philosophy:

Socrates; *"So the soul is more like the invisible and the body more like the visible"*.

Cebes; *"Inevitably Socrates"*.

Socrates; *"Did we not say some time ago that when the soul uses the instrumental body for any inquiry, whether through sight or hearing or any other sense it is drawn away by the body into the realm of change and variable and loses its way and becomes confused and dizzy as though it were drunk through contact with that kind of thing"?*

Cebes; *"Certainly"*.

Socrates; *"But when it investigates by itself, it passes into the realm of pure and everlasting and <u>deathless</u> and changeless and being of a kindred nature, when it is once independent and free from interference, consorts with it always and strays no longer, but remains constant and invariable when busied with then through contact with things of a similar nature and this condition of the soul we call Wisdom"*. [Phaedo 79c-e]

Second quote:

Cebes; "What do you mean Socrates".

Socrates; "I will explain, *every seeker after wisdom knows when philosophy takes over his soul, he is a helpless prisoner chained hand and foot in the body compelled to view the reality through prison bars wallowing in effluence. Philosophy sees the ingenuity of the imprisonment caused by his desires the accessory to his confinement. Philosophy takes over the soul in this condition and by gentle persuasion tries to set it free. Philosophy points out that sense information abounds with deceptions and urges the soul to refrain from using them unless necessary to do so and encourages it to collect and concentrate itself in isolation trusting nothing but its own isolated judgement upon realities considered in isolation............... every pleasure, pain [fear, desire] nails the soul to the body and makes it corporal. [Phaedo 83]*

[Phaedo Penguin Classics *The last days of Socrates*]

To sum up the soul is a prisoner like an oyster in the body tent it must realise that the ingenuity caused by desire and earthly pleasure are the prison walls. Thus, there is an Isocratic definition of wisdom and philosophy caused because of attachment to the physical world of sense perception with the noticeable symptoms of conjecture and vagueness, marked by generation and decay measured and observed by time. In contrast there is the Socratic which is focused on the eternal unchanging truths the natural habitation of the soul by rejecting any sense information.

Erasmus is aware of these differences in "*Folly*" he draws attention to this in several places here are two examples: -

"Farther, Plato defines philosophy to be the meditation of death, because the one performs the same office with the other; namely, withdraws the mind from all visible and corporeal objects; therefore while the soul does patiently actuate the several organs and members of the body, so long is a man accounted of a good and sound disposition; but when the soul, weary of her confinement, struggles to break jail, and fly beyond her cage of flesh and blood"...,

Desiderius Erasmus. In Praise of Folly / Illustrated with Many Curious Cuts (Kindle Locations 1813-1816).

"Socrates in a certain book that Plato made called Phaedo seemeth to agree with stoics, where he thinketh philosophy to be nothing else but a meditation or practising of death, that is to say that the mind withdraw herself as much as she can from corporal and sensible things, and convey

herself to those things which be perceived with reason only, and not of the sensible powers".

"Thou seest how the mother of the extreme mischief is worldly wisdom The wisdom of Christ., but of the wisdom of Christ which the world thinketh foolishness, this wise thou readest".

"Worldly wisdom is very foolishness. Make much of this wisdom and take her in thine arms. Worldly wisdom set at nought, which with false title and under a feigned colour of honesty boasteth and showeth herself gay to fools, when after Paul there is no greater foolishness with God than worldly wisdom He must be a fool in this world that will be wise in God., a thing that must be forgotten indeed again of him that will be wise indeed. If any man (saith Paul) among you seemeth to be wise in this world, let him be a fool that he may be wise The searchers were the philosophers which searched for worldly wisdom yet could they attain no wisdom to save the soul of man until Christ came., for the wisdom of this world is foolishness with God".

Erasmus, Desiderius. Delphi Collected Works of Desiderius Erasmus (Illustrated). Delphi Classics. Kindle Edition.

Similarly, Socrates discovered that the Delphic oracle named him as the wisest man in the world, which he could not understand why because he had no claim to earthly wisdom [Apology 21a] nor does he have any of the knowledge and skills of other people. [Theaetetus 210c]. In keeping with his eternal wisdom, he does not write anything down either. In the Apology he comically tries to find the truth of the oracle's statement by questioning a politician who we could reasonably consider to be Isocrates, he makes this statement: -

"Well I gave a thorough examination to this person I need not mention his name he is one of the politicians ......in conversation with him I formed the impression that although in many peoples opinion and especially his own he appeared to be wise in fact he was not....... I reflected as I walked away: Well I am certainly wiser than this man. It is only too likely that neither of us has any knowledge to boast of; but he thinks that he knows

something which he does not know, whereas I am quite conscious of my ignorance. At any rate it seems that I am wiser than he is to this small extent that I do not think that I know what I do not know".

To find the root of all the double meanings Socrates in the Phaedrus comments that the invention of liberal art studies was introduced by Thoth the Egyptian god of scribes. [Phaedrus 274 c-275b] Thoth he says, *"introduced what appears to be wisdom but was not wisdom itself".*

So far, we can see there is a problem caused by historians not fully grasping there is a different vocabulary between Platonic wisdom and Isocratic conjecture caused by Thoth. Socrates in the great Socratic dialogues always aims to get the sophist to admit that their boastful thinking is just vague conjecture. In the next chapter we are going to investigate why the works of Isocrates became the foundation for Western political thought without people recognising the origin or even his name.

To complete this chapter, we need to be able to recognise a true god from a false god like Thoth. Socrates says a true god does not change shape or increase or decrease as this would mean he was not perfect in the first instance and this would also mean there must be more than one type of god. A true god is overflowing with goodness therefore he does not need to make promises. A true god can never cause evil or harm, God is the cause of goodness how can he generate harm? A true god does not disguise himself or tell lies, Gods do not want for anything from humans as they are the gods perfect and pure. [Rep 377-386]

The false understanding or double meaning of wisdom and liberal studies was introduced by Thoth, Thoth then is a false god and not to be trusted.

Protagoras who is an aggressive exponent akin to Democritus claims that Hermes gave mankind his sense of justice from Zeus. [Protagoras 322 c]

It is well established that Thoth the Egyption scribe god who is sometimes depicted as a dog faced baboon is the Greek equivalent of Hermes the god of speech and deception. With this scattered information we can deduce that Plato considers that Hermes is responsible for the deception through manipulative rhetoric falsifying true wisdom and philosophy. Zeus is a personification of our higher intellect [nous] the eternal unchanging principle, Protagoras boastfully claims Hermes delivered to mankind justice this can only be a justice that relates to opinion and conjecture and not the Socratic eternal justice the true justice which will never change that can only be grasped by nous [intellect] and cannot become physical. Therefore the justice Protagaras esposes is a corporeal justice of conjecture given to man kind by Hermes who does not fulfill the Socratic requirement of a true god.

The Republic teaches you how to recognise the deceptions which are the chains of the physical world which are the sense satisfaction urges caused by the tyrant inside us this tyrant turns out to be personified by Hermes who is the puppeter pulling our strings. Protagoras being a sophist represents the tyrants arguments, the next stage then is to consider the attributes of Hermes: -

Hermes is a false god, he could not have brought the laws of justice to mankind because they are eternal truths and cannot become time related or subject to decay or evolution, he can only have invented his own laws and passed this legislation to mankind.

His mother is Maia the mother of invention. Maya is the Sanskrit term for illusion caused by physical things.

Hermes is the Lycaonian deity, the "Lyca" etymology is indicative of "wolf".

Lycaon the king of Arcadia dedicated the first sacrificial temple to Hermes of Cyllene. [Remember Socrates said true gods do not need anything from humans because they are perfect].

Hermes in mythology he is the god who contrived and invented speech, the interpreter, the trickster, the deceiver of words, the rule setter, the law maker, the messenger of the gods, the escort of the dead to Hades, the psychopomp, the thief, the god of markets, sheep and cattle herders, the god of boundaries and bondage, the god of sacraments and blood sacrifice, the god of deception, a wheeled dealer, a car salesman, a hawker, a peddler of false goods a promiser of ephemeral luxuries.

Being the god of boundaries which are a form bondage, the term religion originates from "religio" meaning that which binds together. Hermes is the god who brought religion and blood sacrifies to mankind.

Plato also defines the nature of Hermes in the Cratylus 408.

The origin of Hermes worship comes from stone worship, statues to Hermes are phallic stones called Hermae.

https://archive.org/details/handbookofmythol00bereiala/page/118

He is also the god of gymnastics known as Agoraios, the patron of gymnasia. [Lyceum]

The marketplace is the Agora.

The name Hermes is indicative of stone or cairn, boundary markers so he becomes the god of travellers and traders.

Hermits originally were desert wonderers.

The Roman equivalent of Hermes is Mercury evolving words like merchant, merchandise, mercenary and mercy

This presupposes if Hermes is the winged messenger and Zeus is of the nonexistant metaphysical realm then it is impossible to bring messages back from Zeus then his wings are also false.

These are characteristics of Hermes, he is a downward force, the psychopompos.

The recognisable traites of the character of Hermes are people who want physical control of laws, boundaries and money or honours (whatever happens to be the merchandise they worship).

Keeping these attributes in mind the next task is to contrast Hermes liberal arts with the upward force of the true liberating studies of Socrates, but first this is a good point to discuss the erronious reading of the Republic that has perpetuate the myth of *the wives and children dialogue* mentioned in the last chapter.

To remind you we are considering why academics commonly miss read the Republic associating the political state Plato describes in speech with real political proposals of the eternal state [Callipolis] which means to behold the "Idea of the good"

Taking this in stages: -

1) Socrates makes the important statement to Adeimantus "that it can never be just to harm anyone, because of the harmful effect it does to your soul". [Rep 335e]

Arguing against this is Adeimantus, who holds the Isocratic views on "speech" and gives the longest speech in the whole Republic supporting "speech". [362e -367e].

From which here are a couple of interesting traits identifiable with tyrants: -

"I with justice or with crooked deceits scale the higher wall where I can fortifie myself all around and live out my life".

"But if I'm unjust, but have provided myself with a reputation for justice a divine life is promised".

[Rep 365b]

2) Socrates to back up his statement is charged with designing a city in "speech" this city becomes a city in feaver/sickness. Therefore the Republics political proposals are for a diseased state.[Rep 372e] not a Callipolis at this stage.

3) Socrates describes the educational proposals for the sick city in speech with Adeimantus: -

Socrates *"By Zeus then my dear Adeimantus it mustn't be given up if it turns out to be quite long"*.

Adeimantus *"No it mustn't"*.

Socrates *"Come then like men telling tales in a tale at their leisure let's educate them in speech"*

Adeimantus *"We must"*

Socrates *"What is the education? Isn't it difficult to find a better one than that discovered over a great expanse of time? It is of course gymnastics for the body and music for the soul"*.

Adeimantus *"Yes, it is"*.

Socrates *"Won't we begin by educating in music before gymnastics"*.

Adeimantus *"Of course"*

Socrates *"You include speeches in music don't you"*.

Adeimantus *"I do"*.

Socrates *"Do speeches have a double form, the one truer the other false"*.

Adeimantus *"Yes"*

Socrates *"Must they be educated in both, but first in the false"*.

Adeimantus *"I don't know what you mean?"*

[Rep 357d-e]

4) From this you can see Socrates is being the devil's advocate, suggesting to Adeimantus [alias Isocrates] how he will build this sick diseased state of "speech" and the education programmes which are agreeable to Adeimantus.

5) Consider: the designs for the city in "speech" just quoted was on page 54, book two, the dialogue progresses all the while further designing a city around the studies of music and gymnastics including Thomas More's

favoured book five, when we arrive at book seven page 200, Socrates dismisses the studies of music and gymnastics as worthless.[The book ends at page 303]

Result; all the political proposals for what the scholars mistakenly called the Callipolis are scrapped, Socrates says they are worthless. The internet is full of academics including Wegemer quoting the pros and cons of Plato's political system and everything is scrapped. Socrates rejects the lot. [see proviso in notes below]

Which means everything that Thomas More found agreeable with Plato for his Utopia is scrapped the reasons why he rejects gymnastics and music studies are: -

Gymnastics he says are a engaged in coming into being and passing away, which over sees growth and decay of the body. [Rep521e] *"this cannot be the study we are seeking"*.

Glaucon asks "Is it music then?".

Music Socrates says *"is a kin to the habit of speech and speeches and there is nothing in it to produce the good we are now seeking"* [Rep 522].

Socrates adds *"The true studies summon the intellect* [nous] *and not sensations"* [Rep 523b].

Socrates further rejects the liberal arts studies as illiberal they bond the soul to the body: -

"All arts are directed to human opinions and desires, or to generation and composition, or to care of what is growing or put together "[Rep 533b]

6) Then we must consider the study of music, the original Greek word is *mousike* which includes music, the playing of musical instruments but also the muses which form the study of liberal arts. These are all rejected, in favour of the eternal intellect like we found with Cicero, Seneca, Erasmus, and the other Eastern philosophes. The big question dare we ask "does Jesus say the same"?

Keeping that in mind for later now is the time to consider how Socrates describes the true liberation studies which will completely confuse you: -

The true liberating art studies Socrates defines as the five essential mathematical studies: calculation, geometry, solid geometry, astronomy and harmony. [Rep 522c-534]

1)   Calculation: Socrates says forget the tradesman use of this study for buying and selling which merchants think it is, it is a realisation that everything is "One" not multitude or visible and tangible bodies. Socrates means it is a metanoia decision to use calculation not has tradesmen or hucksters enticing you to buy into physical things, but for a metaphorical warfare against agrandisment and letting the soul become rebellious allowing it to turning around from generation towards truth and real "Being".

2)   Geometry: Socrates says all those war studies, pitching tents, long marches, gathering armies, drawing line, marshalling troops, assaulting strongholds. It is ridiculous there nothing to do with geometry. Geometry is the study which compels the soul to turn around to look at real "Being" and knowing away from sounds and speech.

3)   Solid Geometry: he says nobody studies it, it is a despised subject, too difficult to find any practitioners because everyone has such high opinions of themselves if you could find someone no one would listen to him. However, both Socrates and Glaucon agree it is a charming subject.[they refer to the study love and affection]

4)   Astronomy: Star gazing is useless; astronomy compels the soul to look away from the things here to the invisible that "is". Using the natural power of the soul reason and intellect Astonomy is the same study as Geometry to look at real "Being" to see the movements of real slowness, real speed in true number, in true figures and how they move one another which in turn moves what is contained in them.

5)   Harmony is not the skill of tuning and developing ears for fine notes and harmonies it is to study the community and kinship between the studies for the purpose of seeking the beautiful and good.

Socrates concludes by adding the comprehensive dialectic study of justice which is the coping stone. [A coping stone is the top weathering stone of a wall or parapet]. The people who don't study this are he says vicious, despicable, or thoroughly disliked persons and dishonour philosophy.

We can conclude that the *studia humanitatis is the study of the eternal real "Being"* which Erasmus, Cicero and Seneca refer and that historians need to be careful and not cast the word "humanist" around loosely. If they do use the word "humanism" then you can define if this is Socratic or Isocratic humanism.

Out of interest before we leave this chapter these are Socrates views on education using his defined studies: -

 Socrates " *Well then the study of calculation and geometry and all the preparatory education required for dialectic must be put before them as children, and the method of teaching must not be given the aspect of a compulsion to learn"*

Glaucon *"Why"*

Socrates *"Because"* I said *"the free man ought not to learn any study by slavery. Forced labors performed by the body don't make the body and worse, but no forced study abides in a soul".*

Glaucon *"True".*

Socrates *"Therefore you best of men don't use force in training the children in the studies, but rather play. In that way you can also better discern what each is naturally directed towards".* [Rep 536d-e]

Socrates the midwife is really refering taking care of our intellect our mental "thoughts" [nous] which are our children, but the analogy applies equally to any learning. Socrates is suggesting, the type of learning introduced by Nicholas of Cusa *devotio moderna*, a Montessori type learning some two thousand years earlier.

But what is the study of the eternal "real Being" that Socrates refers too? We will have to wait for the next chapter to find the answer.

Notes

The above conversations of Socrates on the "city in speech"came from the Allan Bloom translation of the Republic.

For general information on the origin of humanism and its history follow the BBC link, you will also be now wiser than the presenters.

https://www.bbc.co.uk/programmes/p00547bk Humanism.

In the sick state all musical instruments are banned except the lyre and the cithara [Rep 399d] later developments of these instruments are the guitar and the lute.

The true Callipolis is the beautiful state of moksha a metaphysical state of nothingness sometimes called bliss or heaven or even the kingdom of god. Socrates says this society it is doubtful it will ever exist on Earth it is a pattern in the heavens [Rep 592a-b]. Socrates says philosophers despise public office and will never become politicians. [Rep 521b] See also the Theatetus.

Proviso: All the political proposals regarding music and physical education are scrapped however there is an esoteric understanding for us to separate from the literal, for example one proposal is that "wives and children are to be held in common".- The esoteric understanding is that the true philosopher becomes married to Sophia their children are the nurtured beautiful thoughts.

Folly

Facing up to the criticisms of his newly published *Encomium Moriae* [In praise of folly] Erasmus reacted with his usual style: -

I could not have dreamt that " Moria " would have provoked so much anger. I abhor quarrels and would have suppressed the thing could I have foreseen the effect it would produce. But why should monks and theologians think themselves so much injured? Do they recognise their portraits?

His response was noticeably absent of any anger and whilst he is seemingly apologetic, he is not. Erasmus famously said "*I concede to no one"* he had no intentions of withdrawing *folly* which since its launch in 1515 it has never been out of print.

John 13; 34 *"I give you a new command: love one another. As I have loved you, so you must love one another. 35 By this everyone will know that you are my disciples, if you love one another".*

Is the function of wetness to cause dryness?

Can anything which is not harmful cause harm?

Can anything that does no harm do evil?

Then it is not the function of a just man to harm his friends or his enemies or anyone else.

Socrates [Rep 335d]

Deuteronomy 20; 10 "*When you march up to attack a city, make its people an offer of peace. 11 If they accept and open their gates, all the people in it shall be subject to forced labour and shall work for you. 12 If they refuse to make peace and they engage you in battle, lay siege to that city. 13 When the Lord your God delivers it into your hand, put to the sword all the men in it. 14 As for the women, the children, the livestock and everything else in the city, you may take these as plunder for yourselves. And you may use the plunder the Lord your God gives you from your enemies. 15 This is how you are to treat all the cities that are at a distance from you and do not belong to the nations nearby*".

While visiting England the wisest humanist in the Latin world enjoyed the exclusive hospitably of Thomas More's family home in Bucklersbury all the while he was busily writing his latest satire *In Praise of Folly.*

In Latin "moriae" meaning folly Erasmus turns this into a pun on the name of More thus he dedicated the book to Thomas More even naming him to be its guardian and patron. The book begins with an introduction addressed to Thomas More, Erasmus with great felicity reminiscent of the of the TV presenter Eamonn Andrews and his red book *This is your life.* He says I dedicate this book to you; the book is yours now, own it this is what you are Thomas More, you are the last fool in the world to know you are Thomas Moriae.

The heroine of the satire Judge Folly gathers together all the dignitaries of Christendom there she sits sermonising on her mocking stool "you praise God this; you praise God for that; but not one of you have the common decency to praise me and it is "I" the Goddess Folly who arranges all these follies for you".

The bold audacity blatantly under the roof of Judge More, through the medium of Judge Folly Erasmus comically chastises all the devout practices of devotion which More supports; condemning the pomp and ceremonial splendour as outward deceptions of self-flattery, corrupt administrative machines, perfectly designed tools developed for extortion and bribery, become combine harvesters of money, driven by clerical orators, rhetoricians, poetic liars, naming the operators to be the Pope, cardinals, bishops, monks, priest, kings, princes, judges, lawyers. They are all hypocritical brain sick manipulators instilling fear and superstition with the devious dexterous skills of a fox. Folly proclaims Christ's church is founded with nothing but blood and governed by the sword.

Judge Folly is not in the least concerned that men do not build temples to her,

"Yet what do they beg of these saints but what belongs to folly? But no man, you'll say, ever sacrificed to Folly or built me a temple..... as I said before, I cannot but wonder at the ingratitude"

"why should I desire a temple" she exclaims *"when man as made the whole world my temple and it is a goodly one"* Nor she says *"am I yet so foolish as to not know men don't love me, desire me, never refuse me and will always hold me dearest to their hearts"*.

"Folly is not wisdom, folly is madness" she exclaims.

Its serious satirical fun on the institution Thomas More supported, if we carefully examine between the lines of the opening address Erasmus is unashamedly ridiculing Thomas More including the administration and its principles with numerous jibes at the administration he loyally supported: -

The first thing was your surname of More, which comes so near the word Moriae (folly) as you are far from the thing. And that you are so, all the world will clear you......

.....I resolved to make some sport with the praise of folly......

.......Wherefore you will not only with good will accept this small declamation, but take upon you the defence of it, for as much as being dedicated to you, it is now no longer mine but yours.......

......you in the whole course of your life have played the part of a Democritus......

.....Especially when such toys are not without their serious matter, and foolery is so handled that the reader that is not altogether thick-skulled may reap more benefit from it than from some men's crabbiest and specious arguments......

..... No, you'll meet with some so preposterously religious that they will sooner endure the broadest scoffs even against Christ himself than hear the Pope or a prince be touched in the least, especially if it be anything that concerns their profit; whereas he that so taxes the lives of men, without naming anyone in particular......

....But why do I run over these things to you, a person so excellent an advocate that no man better defends his client, though the cause many times be none of the best? Farewell, my best disputant More, and stoutly defend your Moriae.

[These quotes from *Folly* were taken from Kindle edition Translated by John Wilson 1668. There is no support for More's beliefs in the entire work].

Now I have set the scene for folly, I wish to change tact getting back quickly and simply to the points of the previous chapter. Platonic theology reveals that our souls have descended from the divine kingdom of Ouranos into physical matter and become imprisoned in the mundane world of appearance. Socrates describes this through his theory of *the divided line* a cognitive development of man's consciousness likened to a pillar of consciousness. The theory being man's consciousness has descended into this physical world of primal matter from the divine world, our function in this life is to reawaken the divine part of our consciousness and allow it to return to its cause. The common metaphor used for the soul being a prisoner which we saw in the Phaedo, likened to an oyster trapped in a shell, the soul when reawakened according to Socrates grows metaphorical wings and flies back to the realm of the divine. [Phaedrus]

A visual analogy of the souls journey can be likened to the cycle of water which gives a good representation, water condenses then evaporates and so the cycle repeats. The condensing rain represents the decent into the physical realm of creation generation and decay, evaporation represents the souls flight away from creation, dissolution, to the divine realm of Ouranos, thus the repetitive cycle of water compares to the continuous cycle of human consciousness.

Erasmus quotes the divided line description in his *The Manual of the Christian Knight* [rule five] where he talks about a division between two realms the visible and intellectual.

Let us imagine therefore two worlds, the one intelligible the other visible. The intelligible which also we may call the angelical world, wherein God is with blessed minds. The visible world, the circle of heaven, the planets, and stars, with all that included is in them as the four elements.

Plato believeth to spring ever afresh by the wings of love we must fly up to the spirit., through the heat of love in the mind of men. Lift up thyself as it were with certain steps of the ladder of Jacob, from the body to the spirit, from the visible world unto the invisible, from the letter to the mystery, from things sensible to things intelligible, from things gross and compound unto things single and pure.

Erasmus, Desiderius. Delphi Collected Works of Desiderius Erasmus Delphi Classics. Kindle Edition [rule five].

To develop what Erasmus means by this consider: -

If god is perfect would he exist in the visible world of time related generation and decay or would he be eternal?

If god is eternal, he cannot exist because existence is time based and eternity is not.

Then if we propose that god exists, he must be of our visual world of conjecture were everyone would have an opinion of what god is and therefore there would be a multitude of individual gods all vying for supremacy. Simply; for there to be only one god he cannot exist in the form of opinion or conjecture in the world of appearances generation and decay.

Therefore, God can only be described by *Via Negativa* "that which you can say nothing about" if you put into words what god "is" we are back with opinions and therefore simply to cut this short god does not exist, but he is eternal

This same simple principle of the unperceivable god is stated unambiguously in the Gospel of John where it states *"No man as seen god at any time"* [John 1;17]. The Gospel of John is very Platonist in layout for example in the same way that Socrates defined philosophy as the art of dying an being born again similarly Jesus replies to Nicodemus: -

John 3; 3 *Jesus replied, 'Very truly I tell you, no one can see the kingdom of God unless they are born again. 4 'How can someone be born when they are old?' Nicodemus asked. 'Surely they cannot enter a second time into their mother's womb to be born!' 5 Jesus answered, 'Very truly I tell you, no one can enter the kingdom of God unless they are born of water and the Spirit. 6 Flesh gives birth to flesh, but the Spirit gives birth to spirit. 7 You should not be surprised at my saying, "You must be born again." 8 The wind blows wherever it pleases. You hear its sound, but you cannot tell where it comes from or where it is going. So it is with everyone born of the Spirit.'........*

.... 13 No one has ever gone into heaven except the one who came from heaven – the Son of Man.

To unpack the importance of this verse if we consider the word "heaven" which is a translation from the original Greek "Ouranos". A reference to the etymology of Ouranos can be found in Plato's Cratylus [396b] which referring to the Socratic liberation arts it means *"the astronomers upward gaze"* which Socrates said was to look at *"real being"*. [page 98] "Ouranos": heaven therefore is a oneness with the absolute, a pure bliss, oneness with the "One" absolute real being, literally to be mentally gazing in the presence of pure beauty to "behold the Idea of the good" to "wonder".

Cronus is the son of Ouranos, both names are etymologically indicative of "nous" which is usually translated into "intellect". Nous or intellect are the purest forms of intelligence synonymous with the Platonic non-existent god who cannot be described by words and only grasped by pure thought. This is otherwise known as an overwhelming form of beauty or the most brilliant light of "Being". Nous is the intellect which can grasp the "Idea" of the most brilliant light of "Being" this is the invisible world which Erasmus refers to as *intelligible.* Heaven is the *kingdom of god,* from here it does not require a great deal of imagination to realise nous or heaven is inferring a state of mind a kin to bliss or moksha in which the aspirant becomes united in presence with the absolute "Being" bathed in the pure beauty of the "One".

Really, we are just playing with words there is no difference between Plato's paganism, John's Christianity and Eastern philosophy considering all theologies explicitly indicate we must *love one another* then it is a simple matter of loving one another meaning seek each other's understanding.

Getting back to the theme a further analogy that Socrates uses is the "*Allegory* of the *Cave*", he says we are all prisoner's chained in a cave and all we really see are appearances, images of deception symptomized by fixed beliefs. We must break out of the cave, rebel, grow wings and escape by throwing off the chains of deception ascending the pillar of consciousness to heaven. The Republic teaches you how to recognise the tyrant inside who causes the appearances of the sense deception of physical world which grabs and chains us, then we can recognise the deception and break free and fly away.

Plato's Allegory of the Cave representing the Platonic Journey of Soul

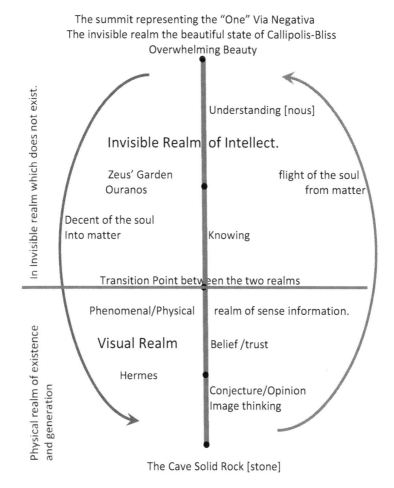

The summit representing the "One" Via Negativa
The invisible realm the beautiful state of Callipolis-Bliss
Overwhelming Beauty

In Invisible realm which does not exist.

Understanding [nous]

Invisible Realm of Intellect.

Zeus' Garden
Ouranos

flight of the soul
from matter

Decent of the soul
Into matter

Knowing

Transition Point between the two realms

Phenomenal/Physical realm of sense information.

Visual Realm

Belief /trust

Hermes

Conjecture/Opinion
Image thinking

Physical realm of existence
and generation

The Cave Solid Rock [stone]

The divided line in blue representing a pillar of cognitive development [consciousness]
Republic 509-511e and 534a-b

[Also, ref to the table on page 137]

Referring to the quote from the Ciceronianus [page 46]: Erasmus said Thomas More was trained into the English legal system which was the opposite of the new learning.

Making a mental note we can add this to a further quoting from the Von Hutten letter: -

He had devoured classical literature from his earliest years. As a lad he applied himself to the study of Greek literature and philosophy; his father, so far from helping him (although he is otherwise a good and sensible man), deprived him of all support in this endeavour; and he was almost regarded as disowned, because he seemed to be deserting his father's studies — the father's profession is English jurisprudence. This profession is quite unconnected with true learning, but in Britain those who have made themselves authorities in it are particularly highly regarded, and this is there considered the most suitable road to fame, since most of the nobility of that island owe their origin to this branch of study. It is said that none can become perfect in it without many years of hard work. So, although the young man's mind born for better things not unreasonably revolted from it, nevertheless, after sampling the scholastic disciplines he worked at the law with such success that none was more gladly consulted by litigants, and he made a better living at it than any of those who did nothing else, so quick and powerful was his intellect.

To which Erasmus in profound Socratic humour adds the following: -

Formerly he disliked Court life and the company of princes, for the reason that he has always had a peculiar loathing for tyranny, just as he has always loved equality. (Now you will hardly find any court so modest that has not about it much noisy ostentation, dissimulation and luxury, while yet being quite free of any kind of tyranny.)

It is reasonable to confer Thomas More became disciplined to the dissimulations of the English legal system through his scholastic discipline. We can also detect from the Von Hutten letter that the wealthy nobility are the military and political leaders that have undergone a scholastic training. The Tudor legal system was an Isocratic legacy from the Norman invasion and Erasmus tells us that it is a tyrannical profession opposed to the new learning.

Typically, an Isocratic education in rhetoric his students will learn to speak well which is the surest index of a sound understanding validating automatically "speech" itself as truth and law. He argues that by cleaver use of eristic speeches to express opinions he will be able to convince a crowd or audience of the truth of his speech, it is an irrelevance whether the opinion is correct or not, which makes his rhetoric a game of deceptive lies. In practice trained Isocratic mercenaries pick up on the crowd behaviour and aim to please them, just when he has them in the palm of his hand then he can make any political conviction into a claim for justice. Justice which Isocrates claims is whoever masters this talent, gains all the qualities that make the truly educated man one who can succeed in life more than anyone else. Isocratic justice is the truth of "speech", and this becomes the just laws.

Young Thomas More is still praised by his admirers for his abilities in the art of oratory and persuasive arguments at public gatherings; in the words of Erasmus we can say he was practicing his eristic *Isocratic rhythm and logical subtlety in the marketplace.*

Laws we all know are ephemeral, the highly paid game of lawyers and barristers is to invent new ways of removing the old ones, replacing them with stylish newly fashioned ones, Socrates in 400BC likens this to a hydras head [Rep 426e]. Unlike Platonic philosophy which there is only one law that of eternal truth.

Erasmus published two books with very close sounding names *Manual of a Christian Knight* often shortened to *Enchiridion* [which also means dagger or sword] and *The Education of a Christian Prince.*

Like a good doctor Erasmus is not just fighting the sickness of Christian hypocrisy he is diagnosing the cause of the disease. Which leads us back to the fundamental principle of *The Education of a Christian Prince* which was written specifically to advise the new prince Charles V of France that Isocrates teaching are tyrannical. In the book Erasmus contrasts this dogma with the peaceful Platonic philosophy he espouses. Suggesting to the impressionable young Prince that whilst Alexander the Greats empire was vast and exciting it was also made with human blood and really was not great.

Erasmus states at the onset of his Education of a Christian Prince, *I have taken Isocrates work on the principles of government and translated them into Latin, and in competition with him I have added my own arranged as it were in aphorisms for the reader's convenience but with considerable differences from what he laid down.*

His evidence is suggesting that Thomas More and collectively the English aristocracy owe their wealth, power and status in some form to the practice of laws which makes them upholders of a tyrannical administered state built on Isocratic principles.

Tudor ideology derived through the legacy of the Norman conquests and held it was the legitimate right to govern by *absolute rule of the king* who was even considered to be of divine decent. John Milton had this same view that William the Conqueror and the Normans introduced a form of state suppression in the guise of Judeo-Christianity. Unfortunately, although his attempt at political reformation made improvements, he unwittingly replaced one form of dogmatic Isocratic oppression for another form of Isocratic tyranny. Even the holy grail of modern political systems, Democracy is a form of tyranny, when analysed it is a collective of tin pot tyrants all getting their own way in which the weaker loses out every time. When assessed properly it is a form of sleight of hand draconian slavery if we consider how this tinny self-aggrandisement is wrecking the weaker elements of our planet. Isocratic doctoring remained the standard for public schools even to the present day repeating and reinforcing chauvinist segregation of Sophia. The Norman conquests spread throughout Latin Europe and even instigated religious crusades into the Middle East. The repercussions of this ignorant barbarism are still rebounding.

To understand the ideology of Isocrates it is best to consider him as an exponent of herd mentality, like a bull in a field of cows. His training is how to become a better bull for the farmer. Isocrates believes the art of rhetoric, speaking eloquently is the key controlling power and exercising rule over a multitude. He prefers absolute control by monarchy especially in war, in which discipline can be as harsh as necessary. If we think of the Great war as a plague its waste of young lives, the human suffering, the shell shocked victims, the unnecessary suffering of animals and disregard for the Earth we can instantly recognise the influence of Isocrates ignorant Minotaur mentality prepared to destroy everything good in the world by serving the master who serves the master called self-importance. An ideology formed by observing animal behaviour the instinct of survival of the fittest, it is insane madness a terminally ill disease of the mind which Erasmus said took many years of hard work to instil this discipline. In other words, it is not natural for human beings to be trained to behave in this demented mad way.

To Nicocles he writes: -

 Not only in matter of ordering routine and daily occurrence do monarchies excel but in war they have compassed every advantage for in raising troops and landing them so as to mislead and fore stall the enemy and in winning people over, now by persuasion, now by force, now by bribery, now by other means of conciliation one man rule is more efficient than the other forms of government. [Nicoles 22]

Paradoxically proof of his advice comes in the same passage which he employs the classic finger pointing tyrants tactic of the noble lie citing the decline of other states of the period are due to them being tyrannical. The above quote from Nicoles demonstrates that he is prepared to stop at nothing to ensure the state survives leaving the weaker by the way side, but he does not consider this to be deceitful, nor the encouragement of others to do the same, it is legitimate, justified and moral - not do so in his book is the immoral thing.

Colonial Empires were built in blood on the principles of his noble lie supported by a tradition of public-school boys saturated in the dogmas. Referring to the Education of a Christian Prince Erasmus would consider it the Great British lie, but the lie does not stop it still continues internationally unabated.

Thomas More if you recall commissioned a monumental epitaph for his own honour this is the typical Isocratic symbol of immortality, it is a great honour to become an immortal "stone" a god of Democritus an hermae [refer to the base of the pillar of consciousness, the soul is dragged into the bed rock] and we can all see the imitation of these hermae on the streets of our cities. Thomas Mores Isocratic influence can be detected in how he perceives himself to be the perfect magnanimous man, *gracious to nobility*, however in his own mind he sees the action of being *grievously hurtful* to his other fellow humans to be perfectly justified simply because they are of a lower class and therefore expendable atoms. His mentality stems from the jungle where you observe the weaker animals of a herd being picked off by the predators. Isocratic logic is just a more refined observation of herd mentality, but it still supports survival of the fittest which includes despicable policy of deliberately making the competitors weaker. Quoting Erasmus from the Hutten letter, *"None is less guided by the opinion of the herd, but again none is less remote from the common feelings of humanity"*.

Although the original impetus against monastic life came from the humanist Gimistos Plethon the call for an end to monastic life was a protest initiated by Erasmus who had first-hand experiences making his escape whilst still a young man. His works particularly *The Manual of a Christian Knight* and *In Praise of Folly* are written to provoke a reformation in monastic life which breeds and preserves the infection of chauvinist misogamy. Consider the sequence of the system perpetuating monastic education using monks schooled in Aristotle and Isocrates dogmas they become the next generation of schoolteachers passing on their mistaken ideologies to the next generation of pupils who maintain the power and control. Gimistos Plethon viewed the future for mankind was to totally reject this monastic dogma leaving no trace of it in our mental psyche, but the remnants are still there in a multitude of disguises.

The walled monasteries often appear to be a benevolent refuge to the grateful poor by offering them labouring work on the estates in exchange for safe bed and board; the same school of thought was applied to sugar plantations. Often, we have a rosy romantic idealism of monastic quaintness, what harm were they doing anyway; we slip into a nostalgic belief, lamenting the destruction of the monasteries and the iconoclast deformation of religious buildings as acts of gross belligerent vandalism, which belies the truth. There is no need for regret, a manipulative state system had evolved from the Norman Rollo to William the Conqueror onto the Plantagenet then to the Tudor and Stuart tyrannies which were fabricated to sustain a very privileged nobility class, the monasteries were there as civil administration centres to ensure the peasants live a peaceful contented existence serving God and their godly king, without any suspicion of malpractice all completely packaged under Gods divine guidance, the necessary preparation for a good god fearing Christian would be the carrot of relief and reward in the afterlife, neat Christian marketing. The poor were deliberately made weaker by denying them any education to make them become placid domesticated animals. We all would like a contented meadow pasture existence this is the trap of romantic idealism and the cause of bondage it is not real there will always be dukkha. The Isocratic system was created with deliberate malice to ensure the poor were doing God's work for their divinely inspired tyrant the narcissistic king. Why else was there a need for fortified castles which gave him protection from his loyal subjects. History records there were numerous attacks on monasteries, conveniently called peasant revolts looting rioters indecently attacking the sundry places of Christendom. The records also record the ringleader's were publicly lynched on the orders from the Abbott or the divine king. In truth this was an organised administrative system for distribution of state propaganda, a brainwashing social mechanism for implanting superstition and mental submission; instilling fears of death, eternal damnation spooking impoverished minds. A clerical hierarchy of witch doctors staged theatrical voodoo spell recitals, dressed for pomp in elegant costumes, ceremonial gaudy gowns and frocks, topped with dunces caps, swinging drug infused potions, parading ghostly marionettes, chanting strange Latin incantations, performing magical sorcery on sacred sacrificial altars, it all must have appeared to the illiterate peasants like Martians had landed from outer space possessing super telepathic powers for contact with wrathful deities who would curse and sentence you to the devils inferno for the slightest misplaced thought. Religious buildings plastered with enormous images of purgatory, fears of Beelzebub and his devils, witches and hob goblins all the evils of hell fire and its many sore punishments deliberately placed to terrify particularly the women and children. Their frustrations and worry could not be reconciled because the law was Latin and only the Pope was the legal interpreter. A cosy informant arrangement covertly carried out in privacy cubicles provided an innocent spy network for the inquisition masters to swiftly pounce on an ever mentally defeated poor. Thankfully Thomas Cromwell took it on and smashed it.

Above Hell and Heaven Medieval stain glass panels recovered Reformation debris.

[St Michaels mount Penzance].

Erasmus pointed out the corruption and vice within the monasteries was rife, the ministries were experts in money extraction from the labours of the poor which in turn paid for the obscene extravagances of the monasteries. It is a tragic loss of the artwork; but in the same way we do not mourn the loss of the Reich Chancellery, the monastic ruins are a reminder of an oppressive regime that besmirched Christianity. This stone art was to benefit the heirs of the Norman nobility and their repressive administrations calculated to disguise a deviously regressive sleight of hand tyranny. Mankind's progress to become sociable civilised human beings was deliberately vandalised in favour of the more aggressive trough feeding animals. The message is still relevant because the nature of the tyrant is embedded genetical in the human psychology, we just become more deviant "selves" with new global administrative tools even though Isocrates may have been an individual he represents our primordial deviant self. Socrates represents our higher "Self".

Isocratic rhetorical teaching looks to use alternative softer sounding words "take back control" really means "subjugate" as harshly as necessary.

William the Subjugator's Domesday book compiled by the monks who were employed civil servants is nothing more than an inventory on what he owned in his kingdom an administrative account for subjugating his *subject-matter*. The techniques and justification come straight from the Isocratic textbook.

Isocratic advice to the King who rules his kingdom wisely: -

"Watch over the estates of your citizens and consider that the spenders are paying from your pocket and workers are adding to your wealth for

all the property of those who live in the state belong to the kings who rule them". [22 Nicocles]

James R Muir in his book *Legacy of Isocrates* argues that the Carolingian Empire began developing their governance on the teachings of Isocrates. The Emperor Charlemagne started using the clergy as civil servant administrators of his new political doctoring which blended Christianity with Isocratic dogmas. The Carolingians looking for state governing policies developed their empire on a revival of the theology of the old Roman Empire, Isocrates liberal arts profession becomes the educational system for a new class of clerical civil servants. The liberal art education along with rhetoric was intended to give a rounded education; the civil servants would become wise with oratory skills to communicate well and efficiently thereby deliver the monarchs political agenda. The Normans capitalised on the controlling power these Isocratic methods produced, coupled with their insatiable greed it was unstoppable. Violence was seen to be perfectly justified from the Biblical precedence's set in Exodus, Leviticus, Numbers, Deuteronomy including the book of Joshua which are full of extreme violence, incitement, hatred, elitism, misogamy and racism for the purpose of subjugation.

Consequently, it just so happens that our brains are marinated in this ideology, through hundreds of years of sanitised brainwashing, generation upon generation have been daily juiced in fraudulent wisdom, rich and poor alike we are all its victims and we all fail to recognise our folly.

The Noble lie of Isocratic dogma is fundamentally nationalistic, fascist, racist, calling on the common culture of brothers all born of the blood of the land into fighting for king and country together. The principle sacred duty for all his state organisations was to maintain a militarised force against the Barbarians for survival of the state. The Barbarians must not be allowed to take the advantage of improving themselves else they will do the same to you. He prophesied a perpetual war and Armageddon between East and West. Declaring to Philip: -

"throughout my all life I have constantly employed such powers as I possess in warring on the barbarians in condemning those who oppose my plans and striving to arouse to action whoever I think will best be able to benefit the Hellenes in any way to rob the barbarian of their present prosperity. When you are carrying out this action you will rejoice everyone will have without fail their portion". [Philip 130]

Throughout his Isocratic doctrine there is the underlying belief in the justice that the stronger has the natural right to rule the weaker. His domineering rules naturally begin with his advice for controlling children.

"Exhort the young to virtue not only by your principles but by exemplifying in your conduct what good men ought to be. Teach your children to be obedient and habituate them to devote themselves above all to discipline which I have described for if they learn to submit to authority, they will be able to exercise authority over many. Further as such they will gain great privileges and if they don't, they will lose them". [Nicoles 57]

This is policy is put into practice in the following manner: -

It was considered in the middle ages that children rich or poor learned quicker through strict discipline, the common use of rod, birch or even whips were routine teaching aides for the necessary floggings. Learning improved dramatically when whipped until blood flowed from the buttocks or a simple whack round the face with a blunt instrument did wonders to inspire memory. The school master lead by prime example his male pupils; the boys soon learn by imitation to copy his example, *you solve your problems with shock and awe violence*, a well-deserved stripping incredibly improves obedience, gained from self-experience. This beating policy procreates more violence then the teaching objective becomes an education for the justification of corporal punishment in the wider social mechanisms of society. This induction into adult savagery from childhood reinforces the belief that might is right, indeed knowledge is power.

No doubt many enlightened people protesting about this treatment would have been barracked with the Old Testament quotes or something similar which appears to approve of this violence. Proverbs 23; 13 *Do not withhold discipline from a child; if you punish them with the rod, they will not die.14 Punish them with the rod and save them from death.*

The educational curriculum of physical punishment was universally taught to pupils in all the English elite schools, even to boys of eighteen, even exemplary public whippings in the town square the techniques of tyrant's kin to the public lynching's. This form of punishment was the norm for children of the powerful elite, parents who have paid for their education, boys being prepared for the leading administrative occupations of state and society. It is a recipe for mass psychological madness, fostering a belief of corporal punishment which is still considered to be the correct method of correction in law. Is the function of wetness to cause dryness?

On the beatings of children attending schools Erasmus writes an amusing ditty entitled Scholastic Studies: quote.

> *"And you know the Master's Severity. Every Fault is a Capital one with him: He has no more Mercy of our Breeches, than if they were made of a Bull's Hide".*

Recognisably Isocrates influence came directly from the Egyptian scribe god Thoth he continues: -

.... because there has been implanted in us the power to persuade each other and to make clear to each other whatever we desire, not only have we escaped the life of wild beasts, but we have come together and founded cities and made laws and invented arts; and, generally speaking, there is no institution devised by man which the power of speech has not helped us to establish.

He comments further in the Antidosis defence of speech that people who can speak well have truth on their side and that speech is superior to intellect.

To speak well is taken as the surest index of a sound understanding which is true and lawful and just as is the outward image of a good soul….

…..And, if there is need to speak in brief summary of this power, we shall find that none of the things which are done with intelligence take place without the help of speech, but that in all our actions as well as in all our thoughts speech is our guide and is most employed by those who have the most wisdom….

…..And yet, when anyone devotes his life to urging all his fellow-countrymen to be nobler and just leaders of the Hellenes, how is it conceivable that such a man should corrupt his followers?….

….." You observe," I would say to him, " the nature of the multitude, how susceptible they are to flattery; that they like those who cultivate their favour better than those who seek their good : and that they prefer those who cheat them with beaming smiles and brotherly love to those who serve them with dignity and reserve.

Ironically according to Plutarch, he had a weak voice with poor utterance and was timorous, and always wished he could speak well. It could well be he had an inferiority complex and this innate fear of fellow human beings has been forcibly bred into the psyche of Western culture.

To sum up the main points.

Whilst he is arguably laughable unfortunately, he is deadly serious commanding huge fees from his patrons to be taught the false wisdom of his opinionated rhetoric.

An honourable reputation not only lends greater persuasiveness to the words of the man who possesses it, but adds greater lustre to his deeds, and is, therefore, more zealously to be sought after by men of intelligence than anything else in the world

Deliberately his dogmas are devious deceptive dictations designed to teach decisively a select few into developing dominant appetitive traits used for exploiting human frailties without remorse. Obviously one of his trained political sophists could be hired by a King to win support of the population for his policies which would make him richer still. His ideology boils down to a form of animal husbandry, if the poor are kept illiterate it is very powerful psychological device hence the reason why he professed knowledge is power and the stronger rules. Not only are his beliefs the foundation for the Western legal and political systems but they are largely responsible for establishing the core liberal arts studies known and taught today. Isocrates was the war advisor to Philip of Macedon; Aristotle became the educator of his son Alexander the Great. The professed attitudes his dogmas cultured are still the common devious traits found in many of today's political leaders.

I am sure you would agree that Thomas More would want more than anything for us to learn from his mistakes otherwise his life was in vain. To do this we must be honest and firm with our inner lower selves.

The political author Louise L Martz appears to believe Thomas More was a just man, his book called *The Search for the Inner Man* argues that *"the humanists of his day were experts in language but not self-control and that the inner man [More] maintained a higher loyalty and always wanted to be a saint than a sinner"*. He further argues that "More was wittier, cleverer, gifted in sardonic command of language than that of his opponents". Martz is an admirer of Mores vituperate language which he endorses to be exemplary, strangely he even defends his violence as a tradition of sanctified bitterness the common practice of gifted humanists. *"Nothing can be to vile and ingeniously cruel to sling evil doers out of the temple, but the true inner man conflicted with these vituperate writings"*. He then cites an account of John Frith who was burned alive in 1533 for heresy. Frith had been preaching against the theology of purgatory and transubstantiation [primitive incantations which ensure Christ is miraculously present in the sacramental breaking of bread]. A reporter had commented that Frith had said that the hard work of his studies made him "sweat". Thomas More speaking with excellent personal knowledge for the deviant methods employed by Christ picked up on a theme of sweat, making the following authoritative statement, *" I would some good friend of his should show him that fear me sore that Christ will kindle a fire of faggots for him and make him there in sweat the blood out of his body and straight hence send his soul forever into the fire of hell "*

To justify his mode of vitriolic, vile and violent language Martz suggests *"Tyndale is spineless with no gift for vindictive verbal mudslinging and only sounded petulant in comparison; More could perform cadenzas around him, with a brilliant cascade of rhetorical buffoonery"*.

Martz is obviously schooled in Isocratic dogmas; because Tyndale in death must still be humiliated.

Martz further asserts *"Mores vituperation stands out because of his literary power not because of any unusual vindictiveness in his person"*. By this he confidently assures us that he was a master of splenetic Latin and Greek cadenzas.

Thomas More was aware of Lorenzo Valla disclosure of the fraud of the Donation Constantini, which is why the Pope held power over Henry VIII, yet he did not offer him this solution for an option to finding a divorce. Valla also proved that the Apostles Creed could not have been written by the apostles and Dionysius the Areopagite was a Christian Platonist, yet More, because of his scholastic training remained faithful to his master the Pope.

Valla's last work Novum Testamentum ex diversorum utriusque linguae codicum collatione adnotationes (Annotations on the New Testament) was gathering dust in the Abbey of Parc near Louvain.

Erasmus must have had a tip off, because he ferreted them out and published them in 1505 including Valla's thesis on the Donation to Constantine, known as Adnotationes. [Interestingly for obvious reasons Thomas Cromwell had this transcribed into English].

Erasmus then spent several years teaching himself the old Greek language then in 1515 -16 he managed to strike up a deal with the printer Johannes Frobishers by allowing him to print the profitable

Encomium Moriae in exchange he would print Erasmus's version of the New Testament.

His Latin translation included alongside page by page the original Greek text thereby allowing other translators to compare like with like Erasmus's aim was to encourage other linguists to translate the works into their language.

Erasmus dedicated his *Novum instrumentum* to Pope Leo X who expressed his delight, *"not only because you have dedicated it to Us, but because it contains a new kind of science and therefore, We give you credit due to a true Christian"*. It was like wise endorsed by Cardinal Grimani as a *magnificent undertaking*. Thomas More wrote an epigram in honour of the work and defended it publicly against detractors. Bishop Fisher thought the translation should have been a little freer. Erasmus ensured all the major and interested parties approved *Novum instrumentum* what could go wrong?

He had found at least 400 anomalies with the Vulgate New Testament many of which are still held today as being correct. Once the news broke that there were serious flaws in the Old Latin Vulgate Luther flew into his rage nailing his ninety-five theses to the door of All Saints' Church in Wittenberg 31 October 1517 accusing the Catholic Popes of corruption. Sadly, Erasmus's quest for honesty became a power struggle with a plague of religious wars which progressively wrought terror throughout Europe for over a hundred years.

What did Erasmus say that was the cause of so much anger? One major difference he found with the traditional Vulgate was the words poenitentiam *agite* (do penance) from Matthew. 3:1-2. By considering the more accurate Byzantium Greek manuscripts Erasmus changed these words to *poeniteat vos* (repent). It was Valla who originally suggested a better translation was repentance, however his comments were uninteresting and mostly ignored by the literate elite. Repentance is a completely different definition to *do penance* bringing the institutional money-harvesting practices of indulgences into dispute and further still it suggests the seven sacraments are totally unnecessary.

The term *paenitentia* in the original Greek is *metanoia,* which does not mean you have to attend church, pay penance or carry out the sacraments. Repent is an instruction to *"turn around to the light"*, make a 180-degree turn towards the light.

The actual verse now reads: - Matthew 3:1 *In those days John the Baptist came, preaching in the wilderness of Judea 2 and saying, 'Repent, for the kingdom of heaven has come near.*

If we now analyse this verse using the pagan Greek meaning for the term *"metanoia"* we gain a totally different understanding. Metanoia is a compound of two words *"meta"* meaning after or before and *"noia"* meaning intellect or rational mind, [noia derives from nous] so metanoia means turn the intellect around. Using the pillar of consciousness diagram, we can see this means like the Socratic liberation studies turn the intellect around and ascend to the brilliant light of "being".

Unfortunately, Luther was blinded with anger and rage over the despicability of the deception but on the other hand he would not have his Christian church polluted by paganism. He was only prepared to lead the multitude in his puritan way, which just replaced one form of Aristotelian controlling scripture for another.

Erasmus trained himself in philology and was able to calculate how the Greek words had developed which gave him a great insight. Luther by dismissing the past origins confined his theology to scripture he would not listen to Erasmus.

Ironically William Tyndale encouraged by Erasmus used *Novum instrumentum* for the base for his heretical English translation of the New Testament.

Matthew 16;18 Tyndale translated the Greek "ecclesiam" to English *congregation* traditionally this had come to mean "church" it really means sacred assembly. Which perhaps does not seem a great deal, but this translation bore the brunt of Thomas More accusations for heresy and Tyndale was senselessly hunted across the marches of Europe for ten years living has a fugitive from his own countrymen he was eventually captured through treachery subjected to all kinds of humiliating torture and finally made into an exhibition by mounting him to a pole and burning him alive. Thomas More gleefully cursed Tyndale in his *The Confutations to Tyndale's Answer* a polemic witch hunt of half a million venomous words which Martz invites us to admire the frequency of his outspoken vituperative words. An exemplary legacy of vituperate writings evidence that he was a tyrannical judge and lawyer dispensing disproportionate charges overwhelmingly weighted to generate a pogrom of hatred and violence without any formal or informal debate. Seneca taught that anger and violence were an illness that infected others causing contagion and plagues. Paradoxically in the same way Jesus taught he could heal the sick, the lame and the blind all you need to do is recognise that your anger is an infectious disease turn your intellect around to "real being".

Other authors have expressed the injustice of Tyndale's story which is one of considerable sadness, it is a failure of our educational system that most people have never heard his name he is an anonymous figure, a posthumous Nobel Peace prize would go some way to recognise our hero who deserves more credit than any Churchill for saving the nation against the clutch of tyranny. Tyndale is to be commend for the courage and fortitude of an inspiring true Eros whose only sword was a pen and his shield was the Christian laws which failed to protect him.

Tyndale famously quoted *"I defy the Pope and all his laws. If God spare my life, ere many years I will cause a boy who drives the plough to know more of the scriptures than you do."* -

We have a duty to be his common ploughmen and the right to investigate the Bible which belongs to all not just to the professional people who by interpretation declare to profess a monopoly of ethics, morals and social values. The pious religious icon Thomas More and his self-inspired martyrdom hinges on the one verse from Matthew 16;18, his conviction to stay true to his faith in the positive belief that Rome was St Peters divinely nominated cenotaph for the interpretation for Christian worship. The Saints theological reputation to become the De-Facto guardian of men's souls rests on his interpretation of Matthew 16;18.

In the divinely sanctioned and duly authorised *Novum instrumentum* in the comments Erasmus added he could see no reason why this verse should refer to Rome. The brunt of Thomas Mores persecution of heretics and their alleged falsifications of which there is an unprecedented testimony of two voluminous polemic diatribes both embarrassingly shameful without question demonstrating he had prejudicial bull vehement anger to be as hurtful has anyone possibly could to that breed of men. Speaking on personal terms with Christ Thomas More avidly wanted to be as hurtful as he possibly could to that absolutely loathsome breed of nonviolent men, his justification for this action the Church of Rome. Rome historically had become the established centre for the Judaeo Christian faith because the verses from Matthew 16 had traditionally been interpreted to say that Jesus had given St Peter the keys to heaven and passed over his authority to Rome. Rome became Christ nominated Earthly theatrical sacred seat of Christianity, the Pope using the keys to heaven becomes the divine interpreter of scripture. This ultra-critical verse from International Standard version of the New Testament reads: -

!6; 18 And I tell you that you are Peter, and on this rock, I will build my church, and the gates of Hades will not overcome it.

Despite the warning works of Valla and Erasmus because of his scholastic training alarm bells failed to ring in the intellect of Thomas More thus his whole reputation hangs in balance on this one statement. For his belief Thomas More loyally stuck to his faith was prepared behave like a bull in a china shop, prepared to incite violence, advocate the burning and torture men such is this statements importance to his Christian faith he ultimately was prepared to die and in final desperation turn his body into a weapon for inflicting recursive damage on those who disagreed with him there by in death perpetuating further horrific wars and to top it all by this defiance he was prepared to destroy his family through further persecution and repercussions.

To demonstrate that scripture and written laws can be interpreted in many ways by any Tom, Dick and Harry to my simpleton understanding far from drawing up a deal with Peter for the keys to heaven it reads like a rebuke, if I can explain why?

There are three key words to examine "Peter", "rock" and "church", Erasmus used the Latin variants *Petrus, petram* and *ecclesiam* in the original Greek they are respectfully petros, petra and ecclesia. Taking them one by one: -

1) Ecclesiam: The Latin Vulgate uses the same word "ecclesiam" which is commonly translated into English as church, ecclesiastical buildings for example. Modern English translations still prefer to use "church" the original Greek ecclesia is now universally accepted to mean an assembly which is like Tyndale's chosen word *congregation*. An assembly would obviously use a building which is easy to see why assembly becomes a church equally when used in the sense of church it is a sacred assembly. However, an "ecclesia" meaning assembly was also traditionally a gathering like an animal enclosure in the market square [agora] if we think in terms of animal herding where the word was used to represent a walled enclosure, for holding of animals.

Link https://en.wikipedia.org/wiki/Apella

Below the Latin text Erasmus used; Matthew 16;18 from the *Novum instrumentum.*

Link https://cudl.lib.cam.ac.uk/view/PR-C-00002-00009/110

Ecclesia then is a gathering inside a stone square or assembly in the market place the enclosure which is used by cattle herders, shepherds and their flocks relative to Hermes the interpreter of scripture. The Hermae stones dominated the Greek market squares and gymnasia. Ecclesia then sacred assembly is the church of Hermes who is also the interpreter of scripture.

Because of Isocrates and Socrates there is always confusing double meanings, alternatively, ecclesia traditionally was used in the Eleusinian mysteries, were it referred to the "sacred assembly of Demeter" the corn Goddess; Mother Earth used in the abstract sense of collecting an inner galaxy together, an inner cosmos [heaven] which is another expression for Kingdom of God. Which infers this use of "ecclesia" is a yoga concept for opening the inner consciousness and a rejection of corporal body [physical things]. "Being born again".

2) Peter or Petrus meaning stone or rock: Traditionally this refers to St Peter the messenger of Jesus and the Pope becoming his successor the interpreter or translator of scripture. [hermeneutics]

Thus, Jesus refers to Peter being the interpreter of written scripture which is how he is traditionally thought of. This would appear to be a correct assumption because divine law cannot be put into words or described by speech and therefore does not need an interpreter it is indescribable.

The question to ask: If god does not exist how can his laws be written down? They are eternal truths if they were written down, they would change through the development of time generation and decay regardless of any strict enforcement of their interpretation. The very name "interpretation" suggests variations opinions vagueness and conjecture by the act of translation.

3) Petram is translated the same as Petrus to mean as stone or rock some etymologist suggest a larger rock.

The Eleusinian Mysteries were ancient Greek corn celebrations "Peter" was the name for the hierophant, the interpreter of the rituals who read the book of law, twin tables of stone known as petroma. There is also a similar parallel biblical description of two tablets of stone in Exodus 32;19 known as the ten commandments of scripture.

It makes sense if the Petram is the same thing as the twin tables of stone containing the written laws of scripture known as petroma.

Therefore, it reads like a rebuke *"You're Peter the interpreter, these are your laws, but on my eternal law I'm will build my celestial heaven and the gates of Hades will not overcome it".*

With this demonstration I have shown that interpretation of Scripture is a matter of opinion there is not enough information to understand precisely what Matthew infers it is pointless becoming adamantly enraged writing polemics issuing threats and inciting violence. It would have been far wiser for Thomas More to have sat down with Erasmus, Tyndale and Meg and see if they could put their heads together to reach a deeper spiritual meaning which we could have all benefited from. Instead we are here five hundred years later picking up the pieces and repercussions of extremely bad management characterised by unnecessary wars.

Clearly to interpret this verse correctly we need more information for this we could look at Matthew examining in detail how this verse relates to the verses before and after. This would probably be a long-winded exercise resulting in possible greater subjective confusion. I would therefore like to keep it simple, to explain my thoughts, we can find more information in John 1 with an equal reference to Peter being "stone".

Taking it step by step.

Firstly, John 1; 51 the disciple Nathanael gets the important ticket to ride the stairway to heaven not Peter. Nathanael means *"the gift of god"* and your intellect is that gift: of nous

Secondly, John tells us that Moses gave the laws [nomos]and Jesus Christ represents grace and truth [divine truth] thus John infers there is sacred scripture and eternal truth. [John 1; 17]

Holding these two points in mind there are two further verses to examine let us see if we can work out if Jesus does hand over the keys to Peter or he is rebuking him?

John 1; 41 *He first findeth his own brother Simon, and saith unto him, we have found the Messias, which is, <u>being interpreted</u>, the Christ.*

John 1; 42 *And he brought him to Jesus. And when Jesus beheld him, he said, Thou art Simon the son of Jona: thou shalt be called Cephas, which is by <u>interpretation</u>, A stone.*

https://www.scripture4all.org/OnlineInterlinear/NTpdf/joh1.pdf

To keep this very simple and clear all we need to do is examine the original Greek verbs: - *"being interpreted"* and *"interpretation"* one used to refer to "Christ" the other to a "stone". Notice for both verses the translator does not make any real distinction between these verbs, there presented slightly different, but they express the same meaning. The one for Christ does add "being" with no weighted significance, however when you examine the actual Greek text there is a massive difference the two words are literally poles apart.

If we first, consider: -

A stone is a physical thing relating to the phenomenal world.

For the verse referring to Peter to a stone the original Greek text uses the verb *HermEneuetai* which is translated as "interpretation" the etymology infers Hermes who is the god of interpretation thus "interpreter" becomes the selected word. There is no problem with this because *HermEneuetai* is defined as "scriptural interpretation" we can also anticipate how the development of Simon Peter becomes the interpreter of sacred scripture, passing on his authority to the Pope in Rome. Particularly since Hermes invented religion, writing, language and is the god who conveys messages from the gods to man.

However, in defining Hermes on the understanding of interpreter alone the translators are selective for example in the Cratylus Socrates says Hermes *means all activities with the power of "speech"*. [408a] the point he is making is that words like the character of Hermes are deceptive. Therefore, the act of interpretation is subjective, any interpreter of scripture cannot possibly be representing the eternal truth which John says is not perceptible and therefore he implies God representing eternal truth cannot be described by words.

HermEneuetai on this understanding is to be defined by physical things "stone" that can be perceived in the phenomenal world which are experienced through the senses synonymous with the realm of opinion, appearance and belief everything below the divided line as per the diagram above on the pillar of consciousness.

Phenomenal means "things that seam" world of appearance, and this vague definition ties with the character of Hermes the god of deception.

Essentially you can interpret all the scripture you wish; the result in the final analysis is they are just words and nothing to do with the study of the eternal truth which is ineffable

The describable things are HermEneuetai the next task is to examine the second verb John uses when referring to Christ.

This verb when referring to Christ in the original Greek is *metHermEneuomenon* which is completely different to *HermEneuetai*, but all translators assume the same definition and apply the same equal terms all be it occasionally with the obscure suggestion of "being". The original Greek readers without explanation would have instantly recognised the difference, with the odd exception like Paul who was the interpreter of Christ.

The distinction: HermE - neuetai relates to physical matter the primal matter "stone" Hermes is the god of Liberal art wisdom, physical sciences, bondage, imposing the controlling measures of boundaries of laws and sacred scripture even the deceptive trickster. HermEneuetai translated to mean "interpretation" is and can only ever be used in the sense of appearance which even with more information interpretation is always conjecture which is why we need the Pope.

The complete antithesis of this physical meaning is implied with metHermEneuomenon referring to the grace and truth of Christ whom there is no deception. [John 1;47] Once you understand what this verb means it cannot be interpreted.

The verb comprises of a compound of at least three words: *met – HermE – neuomenon*.

Met is meta – meaning after or before and *Hermes* the physical sciences therefore Johns uses a metaphysical meaning for Christ which is a reasonable assessment to consider.

To some extent the original meaning of neuomenon has been corrupted by the philosopher Kant who built his philosophy around his understanding of it. The original Greek meaning of neuomenon is synonymous with Platonic philosophy it means something which can only be grasped mentally by pure thought [dianoia].

Plato uses it to mean everything above the divided line an example of this is given in the Republic: -

Socrates; "*Now consider as we have been saying there are two entities and they govern first the type and place that can be grasped mentally, and secondly of the visible, so I don't give the impression I'm trying to split hairs over the name by talking of heaven so have you got these two concepts visible and intelligible*".

Glaucon; "*I have*"

Socrates; *"Right then imagine a line cut in two. Take two unequal segments and again cut each one in the same ratio, one for the visible class and the other for the intelligible.........* [Rep 509e ref Lobe]

In this extract the translator choses the word "intelligible" on the second instance the Greek text reads "neuomenon", quite simply Christ is neuomenon, something which can only be perceived by pure thought and not put into words.

Neuomenon is something the mind alone can grasp, which is the true nature of ultimate reality "real being" which encompasses the whole of Platonic philosophy of the absolute "One" or "the good", within this understanding it naturally includes Plato's forms or "Ideas" the eternal truths which are justice, beauty, wisdom and truth [the real Beings]. The true nature of absolute reality in Eastern thought this is moksha in Platonism and Christianity this is proving to be "neuomenon".

A further example of how Plato uses "noumenon" can be found in this extract also from the Republic in which the translator [W D H Rouse] choses *"things thought"* other translators may choose "intellected" or "objects of intellect" or "perceived by mind".

 Socrates *"Surly now I said my meaning must appear to be that this, the offspring of the good which the good begat is in relation to the good itself an analogy and what the good effects by its influence in the region of the mind towards mind and the things thought, this the sun effects in the region of seeing towards sight and things seen".* [Rep 508 c]

To understand the background to this quote Socrates is comparing analogically the overflowing goodness of the light of the sun to a child of the sun:: with the "things thought" or "intellected" to a child of the overflowing goodness of the "One". Neuomenon used in this sense is the overflowing emanation of the "One" god. The meaning therefore is that Christ is a child of the One true god, which is what we have always been told he is.

Rouse includes a diagram which that gives a good visual representation of the two realms. [see below]

Stated previously the Republic is designed for the reader to be able to identify the tyrant which turns out to be Hermes but he is not named only referred to metaphorically as the winged drone, the psychopomp [Rep 573a] hirer of mercenaries [Rep 567d] who are mostly thefts, liars and tricksters [Rep 575b] and the whole city lives in fear of such a madness. With a further examination of John there is this same theological contest taking place between the HermEneutai scribes of scripture [sophists] and Jesus who like Socrates disagrees with their dogmas. Examples of the conflict can be found 1,17 [gods laws], 1, 47, [no trickery], 2; 14-17 [throws out the merchants and money changers] and 8; 42 etc.

This warning is also given in Matthew 16; 12 were Jesus says beware of the bread of the Pharisees who are the scribes and interpreters of scripture.

Athena the goddess of wisdom and justice sprang fully formed from the mind of Zeus to become a child of his intellect. Marie Louse von Franz would have been pleased with this interpretation.

Plato's Divided Line [Rep 509d]

Phenomena Realm [visible]		Eternal Realm [Intelligible]	
Sun		**The Good or the One**	
Light and power of the Sun		Child of the good or influence of the good	
Rays of the Sun the child		*neuomenon*	
Things seen by sight		World of things thought	
Opinion *hermEneuetai*		**Knowledge**	
Conjecture	Belief Trust	Understanding	Knowing intellect [nous]
Image thinking	Trees Animals	Thoughts ideas	Eternal truths
Shadows	materials	Mathematical thought	Beauty Justice Truth
A	B	C	D	E

The Divided line works on the principle of Phi the most beautiful of all proportions
CE/AC = DE/CD =BC/AB it follows that BC = CD.

See also Loeb appendix page 105.

In the mid fifteenth century Byzantium mystics began transposing Plato's works into Florence, for the first time in nearly nine hundred years the works of Plato would be widely available in Latin Europe. Imagine the look on the faces of the translators Ficino and Pico as they came across these paragraphs in the Republic. [Rep 361 -2 a]

The unjust man must be thoroughly unjust be able to avoid detection in his wrong doings for if found out he was a poor specimen the most accomplished form of injustice is to seam just when you are not. The perfect unjust man will be perfect in wickedness, commit the greatest crimes perfectly, at the same time get a reputation for the highest correctness, if any wrong doings come to light, he is ready with a convincing defence.

The just man has true simplicity of character, none violent, never does anyone harm, but will have the worst of reputations, a lifelong reputation for wickedness and will stick with this course of action in the face of all unpopularity till death when he will be scourged, tortured, imprisoned, his eyes put out and after every humiliation he will be crucified.

Notes.

Etymology of the Greek word νοούμενον nooúmenon (plural νοούμενα nooúmena) is the neuter middle-passive present participle of νοεῖν noeîn "to think, to mean", which in turn originates from the word νοῦς noûs, an Attic contracted form of νόος nóos "perception, understanding, mind." A rough equivalent in English would be "something that is thought", or "the object of an act of thought". [Wikipedia]

Nous (UK: /naʊs/, US: /nuːs/), sometimes equated to intellect or intelligence, is a term from classical philosophy for the faculty of the human mind necessary for understanding what is true or real. [Wikipedia]

Thomas Taylor: The Eleusinian and Bacchic Mysteries, in the glossary he defines nous: -

Intellect: Greek nous, *also rendered pure reason and by Professor Cocker intuitive reason and rational soul; the spiritual nature. "The organ of self-evident, necessary, and universal truth. In an immediate, direct and intuitive manner, it takes hold on the truth with absolute certainty. The reason through the medium of Ideas, holds communion with the world of real Being. These ideas are the light which reveals the world of unseen realities as the sun reveals the world of sensible forms. The Idea of the good is the Sun of the Intelligible world; it sheds on objects the light of truth and gives to the soul that knows the power of knowing. Under this light the eye of reason apprehends the eternal world of Being as truly yet more truly than the eye of sense apprehends the world of phenomena. This power the rational soul possesses by virtue of its having a nature kindred or even homogeneous with divinity. It was generated by the Divine Father and like him it is in a sense eternal. Not that we are to understand Plato as teaching that the rational soul had an independent and underived existence; it was created or generated in eternity and even now in its incorporate state is not amenable to the condition of time and space but in a peculiar sense dwells in eternity and therefore is capable of beholding eternal realities and coming into communion with absolute beauty and goodness and truth – that is with God the Absolute Being.*

Biblehub link below both verbs are considered to mean "interpret or translate"

https://biblehub.com/strongs/greek/2059.htm   HermEneuetai

https://biblehub.com/str/greek/3177.htm   metHermEneuomenon

The Oxford Companion to Philosophy definition of Phenomena and noumena.

These terms mean literally things that appear and things that are thought. Platonic Ideas and Forms are noumena and phenomena are things displaying themselves to the senses. In Plato's metaphor of the divided line above the line is noumenal and below the line phenomena

The companion references that Plato makes the distinction between phenomena as the realm of sun and noumena the Idea of the good at Rep 517b.

It adds *This dichotomy is the most characteristic feature of Plato's dualism that noumena and noumenal world are objects of the highest knowledge, truths and values is Plato's principle legacy to philosophy.*

For references to ecclesia, petroma and Peter see *The Eleusinian and Bacchic Mysteries*; Thomas Taylor, Glossary section.

The Greek word for truth that John uses is "Aletheia" which implies divine truth [theia - meaning divine] Socrates says this is a compressed form of the phrase "a wandering that is divine", he says falsehood is the opposite of this motion. [Cratylus 421b]

Beauty

Isocrates believes that speech is power over mind, in total contrast to this Socrates the mind [dianoetic power] creates everything.

The Greek word kalon or calon means beautiful therefore Callipolis of the Republic becomes the beautiful polis [city], which can be taken to mean a beautiful state of mind.

To understand the meaning of beauty below I have chosen a passage from the Cratylus the dialogue is mainly between Hermogenes and Socrates: -

Hermogenes meaning son of Hermes, however throughout the book Hermogenes seems perplexed to why he has been named after him, there must be a deeper understanding worthy of exploring but for now let us continue with this purpose to understand the meaning of beauty: -

Hermogenes. *But what will you say concerning the beautiful Socrates?*

Socrates. *This is more difficult to understand...... I think this word denotes the intellect.*

Hermogenes. *But how Socrates?*

Socrates. *What do you think is the cause of anything called by a name? Is it not that which establishes names?*

Hermogenes. *Entirely so.*

Socrates. *Will not this cause, then, be the dianoetic* [thought/intellect] *principle, either of gods, or men, or of both?* [i.e. He means the thinking process develops names]

Hermogenes. *Certainly.*

Socrates. *Then to call things by name and that which names them beautiful are the same with intellect.*

Hermogenes- *It appears so.*

Socrates. *Are not, therefore, the works of mind and intellect* [this dianoetic power] *praiseworthy; but such things as are not done this way worthy of blame?*

Hermogenes. *Entirely so.*

Socrates. *That which belongs to medicine, therefore, produces medical works; and that which belongs to the carpenter's art, carpentry works: what do you think?*

Hermogenes. *The same as you.*

Socrates. *Therefore, the principle of beauty is to produce beautiful works.*

Hermogenes. *It is necessary that it should.*

Socrates. *This beautiful principle is as we have said, is intellect.* [dianoetic power]

Hermogenes. *Entirely so.*

Socrates. *Therefore, the beautiful, will be properly named wisdom which produces the works which we say are to be beautiful, which we are delighted with.*

Hermogenes. *It appears to be so.*

[Cratylus 416b-d]

For this rendition I used a combination of translations from the Loeb, Jowett, Thomas Taylor and CDC Reeve to try and grasp the full understanding.

Wisdom

It is Folly— that, in a several dress, governs cities, appoints magistrates, and supports judgements; and, in short, makes the whole course of man's life a mere children's play, and worse than push-pin diversion. The invention of all arts and sciences are likewise owing to the same cause: for what sedentary, thoughtful men would have beat their brains in the search of new and unheard-of-mysteries, if not egged on by the bubbling hopes of credit and reputation?

Desiderius Erasmus. In Praise of Folly / Illustrated with Many Curious Cuts (Kindle Locations 590-594).

Thomas More was the tragedian paradigm trained to be an exemplary Aristotelian scholastic the perfect magnanimous man who was unable to admit failure to a blind conviction that is symptomatic of sickness and illness manifested in the form of conflicts. Convinced by the propaganda of institutions that induced the terror that tortured and torment his soul making it into a caged beast trained habitually through this institution into defending itself by lashing out with shock and awe. His mind was a convict conditioned in the way some people have a phobia of spiders furiously lashing out at phantoms with vicious attacks protecting unnecessary the need for self-preservation. The condemned superstitious institutions he supported self-perpetuate the theology of a dog headed baboon.

In contrast Erasmus, criticised every aspect of these malignant administrations including the ecclesiastical theology which supports just wars, he renounced the inquisition, pointed out gross errors in the new testament, polemicized against ecclesiastical ceremonies including the sacraments, was against periods of fasting, opposed indulgences and it's harvesting of money, was against celibacy, taught that monastic life was senseless, demanded the church permit divorce, mocked the order of saints in the whole his philosophy was a complete rejection of the dogmas of the Christian institution of Rome. However, by far his greatest demand to be found in the commentary of the *Novum instrumentum* in which he called for the Bible to be translated and available to be read by all including women, Scots, and Irish, Turks and Saracens not only for them to be able to read, but importantly to understand. With this he was calling for universal education for all, the ploughman, the weaver even the prostitutes and their pimps non were to be excluded.

This demand for Universal Education Thomas Cromwell was answering until his execution in 1540 at the time he was proposing and planning various injunctions to set before Parliament which promoted a programme for universal education, they came to nothing.

This same universal education was the message that whoever created and commissioned the Nostell composition wanted to send, education for all regardless of class, race or sex, advocating peace, nonviolence. Included with universal education there is a buy product which automatically dissolves the class system and who in authority would want that to happen? The authors who designed this composition not only understood the two theories of wisdom, they wanted to make us aware of Plato's influence on Christianity the future was be an understanding of the "One" god overflowing with the goodness and providence for all.

Along with Erasmus the only people who understood this, had the ambition, the finance and the wherewithal to collaborate and coordinate the task was Thomas Cromwell and Holbein. In the last five hundred years there is no one who understood Plato like Erasmus. The eighteenth-century enlightenment movement only chose to be selective, even Thomas Taylor who translated the works of Plato into English in the early 1800's none of them grasped the significance of Isocrates and Socrates, there is only Erasmus who knew and understood this.

The Christians and Platonists do as good as agree in this, that the soul is plunged and fettered in the prison of the body, by the grossness of which it is so tied up and hindered that it cannot take a view of or enjoy things as they truly are; and for that cause their master defines philosophy to be a contemplation of death, because it takes off the mind from visible and corporeal objects, than which death does no more. And therefore, as long as the soul uses the organs of the body in that right manner it ought, so long it is said to be in good state and condition; but when, having broken its fetters, it endeavours to get loose and assays, as it were, a flight out of that prison that holds it in, they call it madness;

Erasmus, Desiderius. The Praise of Folly (Kindle Locations 1287-1292). Kindle Edition.

Sitting discreetly in the back window is an unnamed ordinary man clearly enthralled with the book he is reading which has been careful detailed by the artist. The actual size is only approximately 40mm sq. and delicately executed. The ordinary man sits reading in the most illuminated position in the room.

The Nostell composition is renowned for its intellectual symbolism and loss of piety which as always puzzled academics the family portrait features several books, the ones held by Margaret Giggs, John More and Alice the pages are all blank, the consensus of thought is that they are prayer books and to have included words would in the period have made them heretical, the artist in which case could have just squiggled some illegible writing, there blank because like their readers beliefs they are barren. Notice the way Margaret Giggs is looking across the room she frantically thumbs her way through the pages. She cannot find what Meg and Cecily are referring too in her book. Notice also both Lawyers hold no books. The only three books which are identifiable are full of Platonic wisdom. Cecil clutches a fourth which is thought to be part of the same Seneca series that her sisters hold. Thus, the three graces take care of the important thoughts.

The first book to consider is one we have already talked about, Seneca's Moral letters to Lucilius [epistles] which is tucked securely under Elizabeth Dauncey's arm as she walks across the room to join her sisters.

Seneca wrote 124 letters about philosophy to Lucilius several quote Plato and he mentions he frequently attended Platonic philosophical lectures. Whilst most commentators put him in the category of a stoic his eighth letter rejects the stoic belief of falling on one's sword and letter 88 previously quoted puts him firmly in the Platonic understanding of wisdom and nonviolence.

 All his letters are available on the link below, here is a selection of quotes I thought relevant to understanding the composition: -

Letter 5. On the teaching of philosophy

4. The first thing which philosophy undertakes to give is fellow feeling with all men; in other words, sympathy and sociability. We part company with our promise if we are unlike other men. We must see to it that the means by which we wish to draw admiration be not absurd and odious. Our motto, as you know, is "Live according to Nature"; but it is quite contrary to nature to torture the body, to hate unlaboured elegance, to be dirty on purpose, to eat food that is not only plain, but disgusting and forbidding. 5. Just as it is a sign of luxury to seek out dainties, so it is madness to avoid that which is customary and can be purchased at no great price. Philosophy calls for plain living, but not for penance; and we may perfectly well be plain and neat at the same time. This is the mean of which I approve; our life should observe a happy medium between the ways of a sage and the ways of the world at large; all men should admire it, but they should understand it also.

Letter 8 On sailing a storm

3. I point other men to the right path, which I have found late in life, when wearied with wandering. I cry out to them: "Avoid whatever pleases the throng: avoid the gifts of Chance! Halt before every good which Chance brings to you, in a spirit of doubt and fear; for it is the dumb animals and fish that are deceived by tempting hopes. Do you call these things the 'gifts' of Fortune? They are snares. And any man among you who wishes to live a life of safety will avoid, to the utmost of his power, these limed twigs of her favour, by which we mortals, most wretched in this respect also, are deceived; for we think that we hold them in our grasp, but they hold us in theirs. 4. Such a career leads us into precipitous ways, and life on such heights ends in a fall. Moreover, we cannot even stand up against prosperity when she begins to drive us to leeward; nor can we go down, either, 'with the ship at least on her course,' or once for all; Fortune does not capsize us, – she plunges our bows under and dashes us on the rocks.

5. "Hold fast, then, to this sound and wholesome rule of life; that you indulge the body only so far as is needful for good health. The body should be treated more rigorously, that it may not be disobedient to the mind. Eat merely to relieve your hunger; drink merely to quench your thirst; dress merely to keep out the cold; house yourself merely as a protection against personal discomfort. It matters little whether the house be built of turf, or of variously coloured imported marble; understand that a man is sheltered just as well by a thatch as by a roof of gold. Despise everything that useless toil creates as an ornament and an object of beauty. And reflect that nothing except the soul is worthy of wonder; for to the soul, if it be great, naught is great."

Letter 14 Again on sailing a storm

8. When you travelled to Sicily, you crossed the Straits. The reckless pilot scorned the blustering South Wind, – the wind which roughens the Sicilian Sea and forces it into choppy currents; he sought not the shore on the left, but the strand hard by the place where Charybdis throws the seas into confusion. Your more careful pilot, however, questions those who know the locality as to the tides and the meaning of the clouds; he holds his course far from that region notorious for its swirling waters. Our wise man does the same; he shuns a strong man who may be injurious to him, making a point of not seeming to avoid him, because an important part of one's safety lies in not seeking safety openly; for what one avoids, one condemns.

Letter 17 On madness and riches

*6. There is no reason why poverty should call us away from philosophy, –
no, nor even actual want. For when hastening after wisdom, we must
endure even hunger. Men have endured hunger when their towns were
besieged, and what other reward for their endurance did they obtain
than that they did not fall under the conqueror's power? How much
greater is the promise of the prize of everlasting liberty, and the
assurance that we need fear neither God nor man! Even though we
starve, we must reach that goal. 7. Armies have endured all manner of
want, have lived on roots, and have resisted hunger by means of food too
revolting to mention. All this they have suffered to gain a kingdom, and, –
what is more marvellous, – to gain a kingdom that will be another's. Will
any man hesitate to endure poverty, in order that he may free his mind
from madness?*

*Therefore, one should not seek to lay up riches first; one may attain to
philosophy, however, even without money for the journey. 8. It is indeed
so. After you have come to possess all other things, shall you then wish to
possess wisdom also? Is philosophy to be the last requisite in life, – a sort
of supplement? Nay, your plan should be this: be a philosopher now,
whether you have anything or not, – for if you have anything*

Letter 95 again on madness.

Having just explained that gluttony is the cause of many otherwise
unknown diseases to our earlier ancestors, he says all of this gluttony
and pleasure-seeking luxury is madness only philosophy opposes this
madness. let them love her; let them desire to live with her and refuse to
live without her.

*Now I declare to you that the same statement applies to philosophy. It
was once more simple because men's sins were on a smaller scale and
could be cured with but slight trouble; in the face, however, of all this
moral topsy-turvy men must leave no remedy untried. And would that
this pest might so at last be overcome! 30. We are mad, not only
individually, but nationally. We check manslaughter and isolated*

murders; but what of war and the much-vaunted crime of slaughtering whole peoples? There are no limits to our greed, none to our cruelty. And as long as such crimes are committed by stealth and by individuals, they are less harmful and less portentous; but cruelties are practised in accordance with acts of senate and popular assembly, and the public is bidden to do that which is forbidden to the individual. 31. Deeds that would be punished by loss of life when committed in secret, are praised by us because uniformed generals have carried them out. Man, naturally the gentlest class of being, is not ashamed to revel in the blood of others, to wage war, and to entrust the waging of war to his sons, when even dumb beasts and wild beasts keep the peace with one another. 32. Against this overmastering and widespread madness philosophy has become a matter of greater effort and has taken on strength in proportion to the strength which is gained by the opposition forces.

Letter 40 on speaking to much oratory

2. You write me that you heard a lecture by the philosopher Serapio, when he landed at your present place of residence. "He is wont," you say, "to wrench up his words with a mighty rush, and he does not let them flow forth one by one but makes them crowd and dash upon each other. For the words come in such quantity that a single voice is inadequate to utter them." I do not approve of this in a philosopher; his speech, like his life, should be composed; and nothing that rushes headlong and is hurried is well ordered. That is why, in Homer, the rapid style, which sweeps down without a break like a snowsquall, is assigned to the younger speaker; from the old man eloquence flows gently, sweeter than honey.

https://en.wikisource.org/wiki/Moral_letters_to_Lucilius

The second book lying neglected and uncherished is to the right of Judge Mores shoulder and refers to Boethius *The Consolation of Philosophy*. The books inclusion is significant, the Boethius story suggest that the portrait was commissioned sometime after Thomas More's execution of 1535.

The story of Boethius in many aspects parallels that of Thomas More's imprisonment and Meg's visits of consolation including their collaborated work called *"A Dialogue of Comfort against Tribulation"* which is known to be their representation of the story of Boethius who was imprisoned under similar circumstances.

The story goes that Boethius was called at an early age to a public career, the highest honours of the State came to him unsought. He was sole Consul in 510 A.D. and was ultimately raised by Theodoric to the dignity of Magister Officiorum, or head of the whole civil administration. Unfortunately, his career ended on arrest, trail and execution for treason in 523 AD.

The imprisoned Boethius begins his story moaning and bewailing his fate distraught with grief, indignant at the injustice he begins writing to take his mind from his miseries. Suddenly there appears to him the divine figure of Lady philosophy her dress all torn and tattered having been abused and raped by tyrants. Through the discourses, she convinces him that with the lost his fortune there is nothing to regret it was all just his vain pride, she raises his mind once more to the contemplation of the true good, presenting him to the mystery of the world's eternal one god.

In his imagination Boethius recognises her to be his mistress Philosophy she explains her presence and recalls to his mind the persecutions to which Philosophy has been subjected by an ignorant world.

From the outset Lady philosophy aligns herself with Socrates listing Seneca has one of those who was persecuted for her principles and names her servant to be Plato.

The book is inspired by the works of Plato: the style that Boethius adapts for his dialogue is reminiscent of the conversation in the Symposium between Socrates and his teacher Diotima. There are numerous recognisable passages inspired by the Memo, Timaeus, Republic,

Phaedrus, Phaedo and Gorgias. Without question Lady philosophy obviously reminds him of the goodness of the Platonic "One" which is overflowing with goodness. It can easily be imagined that Boethius is the imprisoned soul rejecting the poison of self-aggrandisement and preparing for true flight.

Love is lord of all she says lay not your treasures on this earth, what all men really seek is "the good" they fail to recognise this is the absolute good. Providence is the Divine reason itself, seated in the Supreme Being, which disposes all.

"Then, He disposes all things by the agency of good, if it be true that He rules all things by His own power whom we have agreed to be good; and He is, as it were, the rudder and helm by which the world's mechanism is kept steady and in order".

Lady philosophy takes him through the meaning of fortune and fate to show him they are false goddesses and only providence is the true goddess who can unite him to the "One".

This beautiful book simply teaches you "wisdom" to appreciate this you must read it for yourselves, below I have selected several passages which I think are relevant to the Nostell portrait composition squeezing in between the odd explanatory note to create continuity.

All the passages are taken from. The Consolation of Philosophy of Boethius. Jazzybee Verlag. Kindle Edition.

With this first quote Boethius is drawing allusion to Plato's Phaedrus and Phaedo and the flight of the soul.

Lady philosophy says: -

" I will now show thee the road which will lead thee home. Wings, also, will I fasten to thy mind wherewith thou mayst soar aloft, that so, all disturbing doubts removed, thou mayst return safe to thy country, under my guidance, in the path I will show thee, and by the means which I furnish".

"But if the mind, conscious of its own rectitude, is released from its earthly prison, and seeks heaven in free flight, doth it does not despise all earthly things when it rejoices in its deliverance from earthly bonds, and enters upon the joys of heaven?"

Lady philosophy tells Boethius that through his despondency he has placed his fate in Lady fortune she sets about deliberately degrading his self-esteem accusing him of treachery to her true self. [Notice that she says fortune places boundaries].

Truly it is not enough to look only at what lies before the eyes; wisdom gauges the issues of things, and this same mutability, with its two aspects, makes the threats of Fortune void of terror, and her caresses little to be desired. Finally, thou ought to bear with whatever takes place within the boundaries of Fortune's demesne, when thou hast placed thy head beneath her yoke. But if thou wishes to impose a law of staying and departing on her whom thou hast of thine own accord chosen for thy mistress, art thou not acting wrongfully, art thou not embittering by impatience a lot which thou canst not alter? Didst thou commit thy sails to the winds, thou wouldst voyage not whither thy intention was to go, but whither the winds drive thee; didst thou entrust thy seed to the fields, thou wouldst set off the fruitful years against the barren. Thou hast resigned thyself to the sway of Fortune; thou must submit to thy mistress's caprices. What! art thou verily striving to stay the swing of the revolving wheel? Oh, stupidest of mortals, if it takes to standing still, it ceases to be the wheel of Fortune.'

Lady philosophy further tells him she rules fortune and if he considers wealth and honours are true property he is mistaken, he cannot own them they will always belong to her, from this we can gauge Lady philosophy is Athena the goddess of wisdom.

Choose an thou wilt a judge and let us dispute before him concerning the rightful ownership of wealth and rank. If thou succeed in showing that any one of these things is the true property of mortal man, I freely grant those things to be thine which thou claim.

She introduces the concept of the wheel of fate relevant to the cur dog.

Shall man's insatiate greed bind me to a constancy foreign to my character? This is my art, this the game I never cease to play. I turn the wheel that spins. I delight to see the high come down and the low ascend. Mount up, if thou wilt, but only on condition that thou wilt not think it a hardship to come down when the rules of my game require it.

'Well,' said she, 'if thou art paying the penalty of a mistaken belief, thou canst not rightly impute the fault to circumstances. If it is the felicity which Fortune gives that moves thee—mere name though it be—come reckon up with me how rich thou art in the number and weightiness of thy blessings. Then if, by the blessing of Providence, thou hast still preserved unto thee safe and inviolate that which, howsoever thou might reckon thy fortune, thou wouldst have thought thy most precious possession, what right hast thou to talk of ill-fortune whilst keeping all Fortune's better gifts?

How extravagant, then, is this error of yours, in thinking that anything can be embellished by adornments not its own. It cannot be. For if such accessories add any lustre, it is the accessories that get the praise, while that which they veil and cover remains in its pristine ugliness.

Finally, we may draw the same conclusion concerning the whole sphere of Fortune, within which there is plainly nothing to be truly desired, nothing of intrinsic excellence; for she neither always joins herself to the good, nor does she make good men of those to whom she is united.'

The tyrant who had made trial of the perils of his condition figured the fears that haunt a throne under the image of a sword hanging over a man's head.

With this last quote the sword represents time i.e. the sword of Damocles although this may have some significance to the clock weight which hangs above Thomas More, my personal preference would be that this symbolism is a reference to Tantalus who was sentenced into the deepest part of Tartarus which was reserved for the punishment evil doers there for all his wrongs he had a stone suspended over his head forever in wonderous harmony with his name. [Cratylus 395e]

She describes the nature of tyranny and the tyrant dressed in royal purple robes. Moving on to describe the bondage of the tyrants to passion, which draws inspiration from the Republic and The Gorgias.

When high-enthroned the monarch sits, resplendent in the pride of purple robes, while flashing steel guards him on every side; When baleful terrors on his brow with frowning menace lower, And Passion shakes his labouring breast—how dreadful seems his power! But if the vesture of his state from such a one thou tear, Thou'lt see what load of secret bonds this lord of earth doth wear. Lust's poison rankles; o'er his mind rage sweeps in tempest rude; Sorrow his spirit vexes sore, and empty hopes delude. Then thou'lt confess: one hapless wretch, whom many lords oppress, Does never what he would, but lives in thraldom's helplessness.......

And a further reason for the inclusion of the cur dog below judge More.

The violent despoiler of other men's goods, enflamed with covetousness, surely resembles a wolf. A bold and restless spirit, ever wrangling in law-courts, is like some yelping cur. The secret schemer, taking pleasure in fraud and stealth, is own brother to the fox. The passionate man, frenzied with rage, we might believe to be animated with the soul of a lion. The coward and runaway, afraid where no fear is, may be likened to the timid deer. He who is sunk in ignorance and stupidity lives like a dull ass. He who is light and inconstant, never holding long to one thing, is for all the world like a bird. He who wallows in foul and unclean lusts is sunk in the pleasures of a filthy hog. So it comes to pass that he who by forsaking righteousness ceases to be a man cannot pass into a Godlike condition, but actually turns into a brute beast.'

Lady philosophy now talks of the self-mastery of her wisdom.

For since men become happy by the acquisition of happiness, while happiness is very Godship, it is manifest that they become happy by the acquisition of Godship. But as by the acquisition of justice men become just, and wise by the acquisition of wisdom, so by parity of reasoning by acquiring Godship they must of necessity become gods. So, every man who is happy is a god; and though in nature God is One only, yet there is nothing to hinder that very many should be gods by participation in that nature.'

The last quote above invokes the essential message of Socrates in the Phaedo, which is also similar in philosophical concept to the Brihadaranyaka Upanishad quoted below: -

And to this day whoever in a like manner knows the self as I am Brahman becomes this entire universe. Even the gods cannot prevent his becoming this, for he has become their self. Now, if a man worships another deity thinking he is one of and I am another he does not know he is like an animal to the gods As many animals serve one man so he serves the gods Even if one animal is taken away it causes anguish to the owner; how much more so when many are taken away! Therefore, it is not pleasing to the gods that men should know this. [Brihadaranyaka Upanishad]

The mind of god is eternity which covers the whole of time, Lady philosophy reminds him of the Platonic concept of providence, that time is a measurement of eternity, he only needs one moment outside of time to enjoy eternity and know he is part of eternity. Which is reminiscent of William Blake who must have gleamed his famous quote from the Thomas Taylor lectures he attended including Wordsworth who all at once discovered the "sudden".

Through the guidance of Lady philosophy providence provides the eternal, which is removed from corporal physical things, thus fate which is ruled by time is a false goddess.

'God is eternal; in this judgment all rational beings agree. Let us, then, consider what eternity is. For this word carries with it a revelation alike of the Divine nature and of the Divine knowledge. Now, eternity is the possession of endless life whole and perfect at a single moment. What this is becomes clearer and manifest from a comparison with things temporal.

All the Boethius passages are from The Consolation of Philosophy of Boethius Jazzybee Verlag. Kindle Edition.

Thomas More due to his scholastic training followed the despicable advice of Isocrates employing shock and awe tactics to put the fear of his devil into men this generates pupils to learn from their peers an institutionalised demonic fear. The nature of human soul is not to succumb to the bully if the other man believes he is stronger and his not prepared to submit to the shock and awe, we arrive at a cycle of awe and revenge. The madness of war is anger and Seneca taught that anger is a disease an infection that destroys men which is also what Plato teaches particularly with the sick state of the Republic.

With the parallels between Boethius and Lady Philosophy and that of the predicament of Thomas More and Meg, does the artist suggest that Meg has become the goddess of wisdom surrounding her with a halo of pearls?

On the Nostell portrait the artist uses strong diagonal lines drawing our attention to the third book the only book with words which are taken from Seneca's Oedipus. There is a strong possibility the book is Erasmus's Aldine press translation in which case the pages are consecutive but are printed on both sides of the same page and we would not be able see them at the same time which is a typical ploy of Holbein.

The moral of all Seneca's plays are that "anger" is an illness a madness which destroys a man.

Seneca uses metaphors of blindness to represent ignorance, the tragedy of Oedipus is that he is blind to the fact he killed his father, even when it becomes plainly obvious he is guilty, because of his stubbornness he won't accept thus he is trapped like the magnanimous man by his stubborn conviction. He will not accept his anger is the cause of the plague, Cicely signals with her hands there is not one but two of these tyrants who will not listen.

Seneca is asking us to think outside the box the city is plagued by Oedipus's madness he has even married his mother. Returning to the pillar of consciousness diagram with the visible and invisible realms. The soul is a she which inhabits both realms in the form of Aphrodite the wife of Zeus, Zeus only inhabits the invisible realm the highest intellect, Oedipus because of his tyrannical nature kills Zeus his father and marries the lower Aphrodite who represents carnal base instincts. Imagine this as a light bulb and switch, the switch is Zeus and the bulb Aphrodite, kill the switch and the light goes off you are in the darkness with the same bulb, but the intellect is off.

Meg sits reading Oedipus with her long finger resting on the Latin "Demens" meaning demented madness, raving, foolish, insane, reckless, madness, thinking someone for god sake hit the light switch, the whole of Europe is in plague because of these two.

What are the pages she is reading why has the artist selected them?

The words are from the Chorus one page refers to controlling fate by steering the middle course, the facing page Seneca has adopted the story of Icarus from Ovid's Metamorphose. Thomas More was a lad like Icarus tied to the Earth by the gravity of his faith sadly he knew only too well that when he went to the scaffold his execution would cause repercussions with revenge actions throughout Europe, fuelling the malignant plague which festered and boiled with the pus of bloodshed. For example, take the St Bartholomew's day massacre which Andrei de Loo would have been aware of. In fact, we have had five hundred years of unnecessary blood shed such is this evil this is why we need to understand this National treasure.

Seneca's chorus

Were it mine to shape fate at my will, I would trim my sails to gentle winds, lest my yards tremble, bent 'neath a heavy blast. May soft breezes, gently blowing, unvarying, carry my untroubled boat along; may life bear me on safely, running in middle course.

While, in fear of the Cretan king, madly [demens] the lad sought the stars, in strange devices trusting, and strove to vanquish true birds in flight, and laid his commands on pinions all too false, his name he robbed the sea of its own name.

Bibliography: -

The following books each devote a chapter to understanding the family portrait: -

Young Thomas More and the Arts of liberty by Gerard B Wegemer.

A Daughters Love by John Guy

Hans Holbein Portrait of an Unknown Man by Derek Wilson

The Thomas More Family Group Portraits After Holbein by Lesley Lewis

The Search for the Inner Man Louise L Martz

The BBC radio programme series In our time by Melvin Bragg is very informative on an all host of related subjects.

For information on Erasmus: -

Erasmus of Rotterdam by George Faludy

Erasmus His Life Works, and Influences by Cornelis Augustijn

Erasmus and the Education of a Christian Prince by Lisa Jardine.

Erasmus of Christendom by Roland H Bainton

Then there are the cited eBooks on kindle which include most of his works.

For the works of Dionysius, the Areopagite: -

The complete works of Pseudo Dionysius printed under The Classics of Western Spirituality.

But also try the Shrine of Wisdom series which are easier to read, but do not include the full titles.

There are also several eBook's which again are incomplete.

For Plato: -

Try different translation to see which suits you the best. The WHD Rouse is good value and clear to read, but the Stephanus numbering takes a bit of sorting.

If you are new to Plato, I suggest you start with the Symposium and particularly the speech of Diotima.

For anything else just discover and enjoy.

All is One

 thought it would be interesting to end on a myth called the rape of Persephone that goes back probably the better part of four thousand years and demonstrates that the pagan Greek shaman had exceptional foresight.

One day the young and beautiful Persephone was picking flowers; suddenly she was grabbed by Hades and taken to his underworld. Her mother Demeter was distraught and fearful, at the loss of her innocent child, soon her sadness turned to frustration and then to anger and then to raging anger soon her torment began to torture the whole Earth, everywhere plagues infested the Earth. Where there was once green and vibrant growth there was nothing but destruction and the stench of death. The people in fear for their survival appealed to Zeus the brother of Hades for a solution, Zeus in response challenged Hades for his deceitful actions and ordered him to resolve the matter immediately; the two came to an agreement. Persephone would be released from the underworld, which made Demeter happy again and the people were no longer plagued by the illness and sickness and the whole Earth celebrated in beauty, however like all myths there was a catch Persephone had to return every year to Hades and Demeter was saddened and once again plagues raged the Earth causing sickness and ill health till she returned.

To decipher the meaning: Persephone represents you and me becoming attached to Earthly materialism through self-aggrandisement. Greedy human beings believing the sole purpose in life is fulfilment of self-gratification by grabbing, taking and hoarding manifested in the form of plagues of disease, characterised by famine, death and destruction. The unnecessary conflicts that we cause between ourselves through a false belief in the survival of the fittest. Whenever this occurs Demeter, who represents the eternal truth of real "being" is sad and her sadness develops into frustration followed by uncontrolled anger her sickness is our sick ideas.

The cure of the sickness is Zeus which is our higher intellect "nous" if we use it Demeter will serve us well, but if we do not, she will destroy the Earth such is the prophecy of Isocrates.

46451598R00096

Printed in Poland
by Amazon Fulfillment
Poland Sp. z o.o., Wrocław